The Enlightened Expedition

Thirty Days of Transformation

Sydney Brown

The Enlightened Expedition

Thirty Days of Transformation

By Sydney Brown

The Enlightened Expedition

THIRTY DAYS OF TRANSFORMATION

by Sydney Brown

Published by TLM Publishing House

Alpharetta GA.
https://www.ttpublishinghouse.com
Copyright © 2023 TLM Publishing House

All rights reserved. No portion of this book may be reproduced in any form without permission from the publisher except as permitted by U.S. copyright law. For permissions, contact: info@tlmpublishinghouse.com

Legal Disclaimer: We utilized ChatGPT for help with research. We are making no claims, whether medical, financial, or otherwise.

Table of Contents

Table of Contents	vii
Introduction	1
Day 1: The Gate of Beginnings	5
Day 2: The River of Reflection	11
Day 3: The Whispering Trees	17
Day 4: The Path of Steppingstones	23
Day 5: The Meadow of Visualization	29
Day 6: The Cave of Shadows	35
Day 7: The Sunrise Peak	41
Day 8: The Grove of Resilience	47
Day 9: The Bridge of Forgiveness	53
Day 10: The Garden of Gratitude	59
Day 11: The Orchard of Opportunity	65
Day 12: The Stream of Simplicity	71
Day 13: The Echoing Valley	77
Day 14: The Field of Abundance	83
Day 15: The Path of Empathy	89
Day 16: The Hill of Positive Aspirations	95
Day 17: The Misty Lagoon of Trust	101
Day 18: The Circle of Community	107
Day 19: The Mountain of Victory	113
Day 20: The Garden of Self-Care	119

Day 21: The Starlit Clearing of Dreams	125
Day 22: The Winds of Change	131
Day 23: The Sunlit Path of Joy	137
Day 24: The Moonlit Glade of Reflection	143
Day 25: The Fountain of Forgiveness	149
Day 26: The Meadow of Mindfulness	155
Day 27: The Valley of Visions	161
Day 28: The Canopy of Courage	167
Day 29: The Labyrinth of Legacy	173
Day 30: The Summit of Synthesis	179
Conclusion: The Journey Forward	185
Appendix A	191
Theme	191
Appendix B	193
Thirty Days of Essential Oils	193
About the Author	195
Let's Connect	196
Also From TLM Publishing House	197

Introduction

Welcome to "The Enlightened Expedition: Thirty Days of Transformation" – a journey that promises to transcend the boundaries of the ordinary, leading you into a realm of self-discovery, growth, and profound enlightenment.

This book is not just a collection of words; it is an invitation to embark on a path less traveled, a path that winds through the mystical landscapes of your inner world.

I encourage you to allow yourself at least five minutes of quiet time each day as you read the daily entry.

If you already meditate, you may want to allow yourself the additional time to read your daily entry before or after meditation.

As you turn these pages, you are stepping into an enchanted forest of possibilities, a place where each step forward is a step deeper into the essence of who you are and who you can become.

Allow yourself to read each word for meaning, giving yourself time to feel the journey you are taking with the Traveler. You may choose to accompany the Traveler, or you may choose to become the Traveler.

Over the next thirty days, you will travel through this forest, guided by the light of wisdom and the compass of introspection. Each day is a new chapter, a new adventure, and a new opportunity to uncover the layers of your being. From the tranquil banks of the River of Reflection to the soaring heights of the Summit of Prosperity and Gratitude, every location in this mystical journey is designed to challenge, inspire, and transform you.

This expedition is not for the faint of heart. It demands courage, openness, and a willingness to confront the shadows as well as bask in the light. You will encounter trials, but you will also discover treasures – insights into yourself and the world that can only be found when you dare to venture beyond the surface.

As you take this journey, remember that transformation is not a destination; it is a process, a continuous unfolding of your potential. The path of enlightenment is not linear; it ebbs and flows like the natural world that inspires it. Take on each day with an open heart and a curious mind and let the journey itself be your greatest teacher.

"The Enlightened Expedition: Thirty Days of Transformation" is a companion on your journey towards a richer, more fulfilled life. So, take a deep breath, step forward, and let the expedition begin. The forest awaits, and with it, the keys to unlocking your truest self.

Day 1: The Gate of Beginnings

Theme: Understanding and Acknowledging Current State
Essential Oil: Peppermint – for awakening and awareness.
Scenario: Entering the enchanted forest, acknowledging current challenges and setting intentions for the journey ahead.

Under a sky streaked with the hues of dawn, our traveler stood before an ancient, ivy-clad gate. It marked the entrance to an enchanted forest, a realm of transformation and growth. This was the beginning of a 30-day journey – a journey from being broken and broke to a state of mental strength, healing, gratitude, and prosperity.

Clutched in her hand was a vial of peppermint oil, its scent crisp and invigorating. The traveler was no stranger to hardships. Her journey to this gate was spurred by a desire for change, to break free from the shackles of past mistakes and limiting beliefs that had left her feeling both financially and spiritually bankrupt.

As she inhaled the peppermint's refreshing aroma, a surge of clarity washed over her. It was as if the scent was awakening her senses, nudging her to take the first step into the unknown. The gate creaked open at her touch, revealing a path shrouded in mist.

The path was not clear, much like her vision for the future. But the peppermint's scent emboldened her, reminding her that the journey of a thousand miles begins with a single step. With a deep breath, she stepped forward, letting the cool morning air fill her lungs.

The path wound through thickets and overgrown brambles, mirroring the complexities and obstacles she had faced in life. She thought of the debts that loomed over her like dark clouds, the broken relationships that tangled her heart in sorrow, and the dreams she had abandoned along the wayside.

As she walked, the traveler recalled the words of an old sage: "The forest reflects what you bring into it. Bring your fears, and you will find shadows. Bring your hopes, and you will find a way."

Choosing to focus on her hopes, she allowed the peppermint's essence to guide her thoughts towards her aspirations. She envisioned a life where she was not just surviving but thriving. A life where her debts were settled, her relationships mended, and her dreams pursued with vigor.

The path led to a clearing where sunlight broke through the canopy, casting dancing shadows on the forest floor. Here, she paused, taking out a small journal. It was time to set her intentions for the journey ahead.

She wrote:

Acknowledge the Present: "I am here, at the beginning, ready to face my challenges and embrace change."

Define Clear Goals: "In 30 days, I want to have a plan to manage my finances, start mending important relationships, and take steps towards pursuing my dreams."

Commit to the Journey: "I am committed to this path, no matter the challenges, knowing each step forward is a step towards growth and healing."

As she penned these words, the mist on the path ahead seemed to lift slightly, revealing the next stretch of her journey. It was a symbolic gesture from the forest, acknowledging her intentions and clearing the way forward.

The day's journey ended at a small brook, its waters clear and soothing. She dipped her hands into the cool stream, the water symbolizing the cleansing of past burdens and the renewal of hope.

That evening, as she set up camp under the stars, the traveler reflected on the day's lessons. The peppermint oil, now a symbol of her awakening, rested beside her. It had not only cleared her mind but had also opened her heart to the possibilities that lay ahead.

She realized that acknowledging her current state was not an admission of defeat, but a brave acceptance of reality. Setting clear goals was not just about having a vision, but about creating a tangible path to follow. And committing to the journey was perhaps the most vital step – it was a pledge to herself, to persevere through the unknowns and challenges that lay ahead.

As she drifted into sleep, the traveler felt a sense of peace. The journey through the enchanted forest had just begun, but she was already learning, growing, and transforming. She was no longer just the broken and broke individual who had stood before the Gate of Beginnings that morning. She was a traveler on a path to healing, strength, gratitude, and prosperity.

Day 2: The River of Reflection

Theme: Setting Clear, Achievable Goals
Essential Oil: Lavender – for calmness and clarity.
Scenario: Reflecting upon personal aspirations, setting goals like navigating a river's course.

The first rays of dawn danced through the leaves, gently rousing our traveler from her slumber. The previous day's encounters at the Gate of Beginnings lingered in her mind, imbued with the invigorating scent of peppermint that had awakened her senses to the possibilities of change. Today, she felt a renewed sense of purpose, her spirit buoyed by the promise of clarity and direction.

The path she followed was dappled with sunlight, leading her to the serene banks of a river. This was the River of Reflection, its waters smooth and clear, mirroring the sky above and the soul within. Here, she would embark on the vital task of setting her goals, guided by the tranquil essence of lavender.

As she approached the river, a soft breeze carried the scent of lavender towards her, emanating from a small vial left upon a rock. She picked up the vial, its fragrance instantly calming her thoughts, soothing the whirlwind of worries and doubts that often clouded her mind. In the heart of this tranquility, she found the perfect space to reflect and envision her future.

Sitting on the soft grass by the riverbank, she gazed into the water, seeing her reflection staring back. It was as if the river was inviting her to look deeper, beyond the surface, into the depths of her own aspirations. With her journal open and the lavender oil by her side, she began the intimate process of setting her goals.

Financial Freedom: *She pondered her current financial state, mired in debts and uncertainties. The river, with its steady flow, reminded her of the need for a consistent approach to managing finances. She wrote down her intention to create a detailed budget, track her spending, and explore ways to reduce debts. The goal was to create a stable foundation upon which she could build her dreams.*

Healing Relationships: *The river's gentle flow mirrored the ebb and flow of relationships. She recognized the need to mend strained bonds and nurture new ones. Her goal was to reach out to family and friends she had drifted away from, to listen and understand, to offer forgiveness and seek it in return. She envisioned herself rebuilding these connections with patience and love, much like the river that carves its way through the landscape, slowly but surely.*

Personal Development: *She reflected on her passions and interests that had been sidelined in the hustle of life. The river, ever evolving yet steadfast, inspired her to pursue personal growth. She set a goal to dedicate time each week to activities that nurtured her soul, be it through art, learning, or nature walks. It was a commitment to herself to rekindle the flames of her creativity and curiosity.*

With each goal penned, a sense of empowerment washed over her. These were not just idle wishes; they were steppingstones to a future she was actively shaping. The river, with its calm yet persistent nature, stood as a testament to the power of perseverance and intention.

As the day unfolded, she remained by the river, occasionally jotting down thoughts and ideas that bubbled up to the surface. The lavender's soothing presence was a constant companion, helping her navigate through her thoughts and emotions.

As the sun began to dip below the horizon, painting the sky in shades of orange and pink, she closed her journal. The day's reflections had brought clarity and a newfound sense of purpose. Her goals were set, not carved in stone, but etched in the flowing waters of possibility.

That night, as she lay in her tent, the gentle sound of the river lulling her to sleep, she felt a profound connection to her journey. The River of Reflection had not only shown her a mirror to her soul but had also revealed the path forward. With the calming scent of lavender lingering in the air, she drifted into a peaceful sleep, her heart and mind aligned with the journey ahead.

Day 3: The Whispering Trees

Theme: Understanding the Law of Correspondence
Essential Oil: Eucalyptus – for mental clarity.
Scenario: Learning that external reality reflects internal states, embracing positive thoughts and energy.

As the first light of dawn filtered through the forest canopy, our traveler stirred from her dreams, filled with the resonant clarity she had found by the River of Reflection. Today, her path beckoned her deeper into the heart of the enchanted forest, to a place where the ancient wisdom of nature whispered secrets long held within the earth.

The Grove of Whispering Trees awaited her, an ethereal space where the trees themselves spoke of the mysteries of the universe. Each rustle of their leaves, each creak of their branches, was a language of its own, carrying messages of truth and reflection.

In the center of the grove, she discovered a vial of eucalyptus oil nestled in the moss at the base of an imposing oak. The oil's sharp, clean scent pierced through the morning air, bringing with it a sense of focus and mental acuity. As she inhaled its aroma, her thoughts, previously clouded with confusion, began to clear, revealing a deeper understanding of herself and her place in the world.

The trees, towering and majestic, seemed to lean in, their leaves rustling with the energy of ancient knowledge. "The world outside mirrors the world within," they whispered. "Change your thoughts, and you change your reality." This was the universal law of 'As Above, So Below' — a principle that her external experiences were reflections of her internal state.

Seated at the foot of the oak, her journal open before her, she began to delve into the depths of her beliefs, guided by the clarifying essence of eucalyptus. The exercise was one of deep introspection, a journey into the recesses of her mind where shadows of doubt and fear had long resided.

Financial Reflections: *She confronted her fears surrounding money and scarcity. She had often felt trapped in a cycle of financial instability, her thoughts clouded with anxiety and a sense of powerlessness. But here, in the grove, she began to rewrite this narrative. She penned affirmations of abundance and control, envisioning a future where she managed her finances with wisdom and foresight. "I am deserving of financial security. Prosperity flows to and from me."*

Relational Insights: *She explored the doubts that had strained her relationships. Memories of misunderstandings and unresolved conflicts surfaced, but she approached them with a new perspective. The eucalyptus, with its purifying energy, helped her see these past hurts as opportunities for growth and healing. She wrote affirmations of love, understanding, and forgiveness, visualizing herself rebuilding and nurturing her relationships with compassion and empathy.*

Personal Growth: *Her self-limiting beliefs regarding her abilities and worth had often hindered her personal development. She had silenced her passions and dreams, deeming them unattainable. But the whispering trees told a different story — one of limitless potential and the power of self-belief. She crafted affirmations of self-confidence and determination, picturing herself pursuing her passions with vigor and success.*

Throughout the day, she engaged in this transformative exercise, her mind gradually freeing itself from the chains of negative thinking. The trees stood as silent witnesses to her metamorphosis, their whispers now songs of encouragement and strength.

As the sun began its descent, painting the sky in hues of amber and crimson, she felt a profound shift within her. The Grove of Whispering Trees had not just spoken to her; it had listened and responded, echoing her newly found truths and affirmations.

That night, under a blanket of stars, she reflected on the day's journey. The scent of eucalyptus lingered, a reminder of the clarity and insights gained. She had entered the grove burdened by the weight of her internal conflicts, but she left with a sense of liberation and empowerment. Her reality, she now understood, was hers to shape, a canvas upon which her thoughts and beliefs painted the picture of her life.

Day 4: The Path of Steppingstones

Theme: Establishing Small, Consistent Habits
Essential Oil: Lemon – for energy and focus.
Scenario: Realizing the power of small habits in creating significant life changes.

On the fourth morning of her journey, as the forest awoke bathed in the soft glow of dawn, our traveler found herself rejuvenated, her spirit buoyed by the transformative insights gained in the Grove of Whispering Trees. Today's path took her to a new realm within the enchanted forest, one that promised to teach her the power of small, consistent actions – the Path of Steppingstones.

The path wound through the thick underbrush and opened onto the banks of a meandering brook. Across it lay a series of steppingstones, each one a different shape and size, leading to the opposite bank. These stones, she realized, symbolized the small habits that, when strung together, form the bridge to achieving one's goals.

Nestled among the reeds beside the brook, she found a vial of lemon oil. The scent was bright and invigorating, cutting through the morning mist. She dabbed a drop of the oil on her wrists, the citrus aroma energizing her senses and focusing her mind on the task ahead.

As she stepped onto the first stone, she thought about the small habits she needed to establish to achieve her financial goals. She envisioned checking her bank statements regularly, curbing impulsive purchases, and setting aside a small amount weekly for savings. Each of these actions was a stone in the brook of her financial journey, small yet significant.

The next few stones represented the habits needed to mend and strengthen her relationships. She imagined sending a message to a friend she hadn't spoken to in a while, planning regular family dinners, and actively listening during conversations. These actions, though seemingly minor, were crucial in building the bridge to stronger, more meaningful connections.

Further across the brook, the stones symbolized her personal development. She saw herself setting aside time each day for her hobbies, reading books that sparked her creativity, and taking short walks to clear her mind and gather inspiration. Each habit was a step towards nurturing her passions and personal growth.

With each stone she stepped on, the traveler felt a sense of progress. The lemon oil's fragrance, ever-present, served as a reminder of the energy and focus required to maintain these habits. It was a journey of persistence and consistency, each small step contributing to a larger change.

Midway across the brook, she paused, looking back to see the distance she had covered. It was a metaphor for her journey so far – each small habit, each decision, had brought her to this point. She realized that change did not happen in grand, sweeping gestures but in the accumulation of small, daily actions.

Encouraged by this revelation, she continued her journey across the brook. With each step, her confidence grew, her belief in the process strengthened. The lemon oil's zestful scent was a constant companion, a cheerful encouragement in her endeavor.

As she reached the final stone and stepped onto the opposite bank, she felt a surge of accomplishment. She had crossed the brook, one stone at a time, just as she would achieve her goals, one habit at a time.

Resting by the bank, she took out her journal. Under the energizing aroma of the lemon oil, she began to write down the small habits she would incorporate into her daily life. These habits were her steppingstones, the building blocks of her journey towards financial stability, enriched relationships, and personal fulfillment.

As the day waned into evening, the traveler sat by the brook, reflecting on the lessons of the day. The path of steppingstones had taught her the power of small actions, the cumulative effect of daily habits in creating lasting change.

That night, under the starlit sky, she pondered the journey ahead. The lemon oil's uplifting fragrance lingered around her, a symbol of the energy and focus she would carry forward. She understood now that the journey of transformation was not a leap, but a series of steps, each one taken with intention and purpose.

As she drifted to sleep, the gentle babble of the brook whispered a lullaby of persistence and progress. She knew that the path ahead would require dedication and consistency, but she was ready. Ready to build her bridge, one stone at a time, towards a life of prosperity, connection, and self-actualization.

Day 5: The Meadow of Visualization

Theme: Visualizing Success and Prosperity
Essential Oil: Rosemary – for cognitive clarity.
Scenario: Employing mental imagery to manifest goals and dreams.

As the new day dawned, painting the sky in hues of soft pink and amber, our traveler awakened with a heart full of hope. The journey thus far had been transformative, each day bringing its own lessons and revelations. Today, she was to venture into the Meadow of Visualization, a place within the enchanted forest renowned for its power to turn dreams into tangible visions.

The path led her through the dense foliage of the forest, which gradually opened up to a breathtaking meadow. The meadow was a mosaic of vibrant wildflowers, swaying gracefully under the gentle morning breeze. In the heart of this kaleidoscope of colors stood a magnificent tree, its branches spreading wide, as if embracing the sky.

Beneath the tree, she found a small vial of rosemary oil, its aroma sharp and refreshing. Known for enhancing memory and mental clarity, the rosemary oil was the perfect aid for the day's task of visualizing her goals. She applied a drop of the oil onto her temples, immediately feeling a sense of alertness and focus.

Sitting under the tree, she closed her eyes and took a deep breath, allowing the scent of rosemary to guide her thoughts. She began to envision her future, painting mental images of her goals and aspirations.

The first vision was of her financial freedom. She saw herself in a life where money was no longer a source of anxiety but a tool for achieving her dreams. She pictured herself paying off her debts, one by one, and watching her savings grow. She imagined the feeling of empowerment and relief that would come with financial stability, the freedom to make choices not dictated by economic constraints.

Next, she focused on her relationships. In her mind's eye, she visualized reconnecting with old friends, healing past wounds with heartfelt conversations, and building new, meaningful connections. She saw herself surrounded by a community of support and love, sharing moments of joy and companionship. Each relationship was a thread in the rich tapestry of her life, woven with understanding and mutual respect.

Then, she turned her attention to her personal growth. She imagined herself pursuing her passions without fear or hesitation. She saw herself painting, her brush strokes filled with confidence and creativity. She envisioned herself exploring new places, each adventure adding to her growth and self-awareness. She saw herself reading, learning, and expanding her knowledge, becoming a more well-rounded and enlightened individual.

As she dwelt in each visualization, the meadow around her seemed to come alive, resonating with the energy of her dreams. The wildflowers appeared to dance in tune with her aspirations, the tree's leaves rustling in quiet applause.

She spent hours in this state of deep visualization, each goal being carefully crafted in her mind, infused with emotion and desire. The rosemary oil kept her mind sharp and focused, each breath bringing a renewed sense of clarity.

As the sun traversed the sky, casting changing shadows across the meadow, she began to pair each vision with an affirmation. "I am achieving financial freedom. I am nurturing fulfilling relationships. I am embracing my personal growth." These affirmations were not mere words but powerful declarations of her intentions.

When evening approached, and the meadow was bathed in the golden light of the setting sun, she opened her eyes. The world around her seemed more vibrant, more alive. The experience in the Meadow of Visualization had not just been an exercise in imagination; it was a profound journey into the realm of possibility.

That night, as she lay in her tent, the images she had visualized remained vivid in her mind, the scent of rosemary a constant reminder of their clarity and potency. She had painted a future of her own design, a future where her goals were not distant dreams but imminent realities.

As she drifted into sleep, her heart was alight with the possibilities that lay ahead. The Meadow of Visualization had shown her the power of her mind to shape her destiny. With each day, she was not just moving through the enchanted forest; she was also journeying closer to the life she yearned for, a life of abundance, fulfillment, and joy.

Day 6: The Cave of Shadows

Theme: Overcoming Limiting Beliefs
Essential Oil: Frankincense – for spiritual grounding.
Scenario: Confronting and dispelling deep-seated fears and doubts.

On the sixth day of her transformative journey, as the morning sun cast a soft, golden light over the forest, our traveler set out with a sense of determined resolve. The lessons from the Meadow of Visualization still lingered in her mind, empowering her with visions of a future she was beginning to believe was attainable. Today, she was to face one of her most significant challenges yet – the Cave of Shadows.

The path wound deeper into the heart of the forest, leading her to the mouth of a cave. It was an imposing sight, the cave's entrance shrouded in darkness, a stark contrast to the vibrant life of the forest. Here, she was to confront and overcome her limiting beliefs, the deep-seated fears that had held her back from realizing her true potential.

As she stood at the entrance, she found a small vial of Frankincense oil nestled in the crevices of the rocky threshold. Known for its grounding and spiritual properties, the Frankincense oil was her ally in this journey into the depths of her psyche. She applied a few drops to her wrists, the rich, earthy aroma steadying her nerves and fortifying her spirit.

With a deep breath, she stepped into the cave. The darkness surrounded her, a physical manifestation of the doubts and fears that had clouded her mind for years. The air was cool and still, as if time itself had paused within these ancient walls.

As her eyes adjusted to the dim light, she saw them – the Shadows. They were not physical entities but whispers of her own insecurities, echoes of negative thoughts that had become entrenched in her mind. "You are not capable," one shadow hissed. "You will never succeed," another taunted.

Each word struck her like a physical blow, but she stood firm, the scent of Frankincense a constant reminder of her strength and purpose. She realized that these shadows were manifestations of her own creation, born from the fears and doubts she had internalized over the years.

Drawing strength from the Frankincense oil, she confronted each shadow, countering their lies with the truths she had come to embrace. "I am capable, and I am worthy," she declared to the shadow of doubt. "I will succeed because I am determined and resilient," she affirmed to the shadow of fear.

With each assertion, the shadows began to wane, their voices diminishing until they were nothing but whispers in the darkness. The cave, which had initially felt oppressive and daunting, now seemed less intimidating, the shadows retreating into the furthest corners.

She continued to move deeper into the cave, her heart growing lighter with every step. The Frankincense oil's aroma comforted her, a protective shroud against the remnants of negativity that tried to cling to her.

Finally, she reached the heart of the cave, where a faint light illuminated a small, tranquil pool. The water was clear and still, reflecting the newfound lightness in her soul. She realized that this pool represented her inner peace, a tranquility that had been there all along, obscured by the shadows of her fears.

She knelt by the pool, the reflections in the water mirroring the transformation that had taken place within her. She had faced her deepest fears, challenged her limiting beliefs, and emerged stronger and more confident.

As she made her way back to the cave's entrance, the path seemed brighter, the darkness no longer as daunting. She emerged into the daylight, the forest welcoming her back with open arms.

That evening, as she settled in her camp, the scent of Frankincense lingering in the air, she reflected on the day's journey. She had ventured into the depths of her fears and emerged victorious. The Cave of Shadows had been a crucible, a place of confrontation and rebirth.

As she lay under the stars, a sense of peace cradled her. She had not only overcome her shadows but had also gained a profound understanding of her inner strength. The journey ahead would undoubtedly hold more challenges, but she now knew that she had the power to face them and prevail.

Day 7: The Sunrise Peak

Theme: Embracing a New Perspective
Essential Oil: Orange – for joy and positivity.
Scenario: Witnessing the beauty of change and embracing new perspectives.

The seventh day of her transformative journey greeted our traveler with the soft caress of dawn's first light. The air, tinged with the freshness of a new beginning, held a promise of revelations yet to unfold. Today, she was destined for Sunrise Peak, a place renowned for its inspiring vistas and the profound change in perspective it offered to those who reached its summit.

The path to the peak meandered through the forest, ascending gradually. Each step upwards took her further away from the dense canopy below, into a world where the sky seemed to open up, embracing her with its vastness. In her hand, she clutched a vial of orange oil, its scent vibrant and uplifting. A dab of the oil on her wrists invigorated her senses, infusing her climb with a sense of zest and anticipation.

As she ascended, the traveler contemplated the journey that had led her here. Each day in the enchanted forest had been a step towards self-discovery, unearthing strengths and confronting weaknesses she had never known. The steep and winding path to the peak was a physical echo of her journey, a reminder that the road to self-improvement was rarely straightforward but always upwards.

Halfway up the mountain, she encountered a grove of mountain flowers, their petals glistening with dew. Here, she paused, inhaling the combined aromas of the orange oil and the fresh, alpine air. The moment was transcendent, a beautiful symphony of nature and her newfound inner peace. She closed her eyes, allowing herself to fully absorb the tranquility and strength of her surroundings.

Resuming her climb, the landscape began to change. The trees grew sparse, giving way to rocky outcrops and rugged terrain. The air grew cooler and sharper, but the scent of the orange oil was a warm, constant presence, encouraging her to press on.

Reaching a particularly steep incline, she paused to gather her strength. Looking back, she marveled at how far she had come, not just in terms of the mountain she was scaling but also in her personal journey. Each step upwards was a triumph over her past limitations, a testament to her growing resilience and determination.

Finally, as the first rays of the sun broke over the horizon, she reached the summit of Sunrise Peak. The world below was awash in a golden glow, a breathtaking collage of forest, valleys, and distant mountains. The sight was overwhelming in its beauty and scale, offering a new perspective on the world and her place in it.

Sitting at the peak, covered in the sweet scent of orange oil, she took out her journal. Inspired by the majestic panorama before her, she wrote about perspective — how a change in viewpoint can alter one's understanding of life's challenges. From this height, her problems, which once seemed insurmountable, now appeared as mere parts of a larger, beautiful journey.

The sun's warm rays bathed her in light, reinforcing her reflections. The scent of orange oil mingled with the crisp mountain air, creating an atmosphere of clarity and insight. She felt a profound connection to the universe, a sense of being part of something much larger than herself.

She spent hours at the peak, immersed in contemplation and gratitude. It was a moment to honor her journey, to recognize the growth and change she had undergone. The peak was a physical and symbolic representation of her newfound perspective — a higher vantage point from which the challenges of life seemed less daunting.

As she descended from Sunrise Peak in the late afternoon, the traveler felt a deep sense of accomplishment and renewal. The journey up the mountain had been a metaphor for her personal growth, a physical manifestation of her ascent to a new way of thinking and being.

That evening, nestled in her camp with the orange oil's fragrance still lingering, she felt an overwhelming sense of gratitude. She had not only witnessed the dawn from the mountain's summit but had also experienced the dawning of a new perspective within herself. The world, she realized, was full of beauty and possibilities, waiting to be explored from this new vantage point of understanding and appreciation.

Day 8: The Grove of Resilience

Theme: Building Resilience and Strength
Essential Oil: Cedarwood – for steadiness and endurance.
Scenario: Learning resilience through the steadfast nature of trees.

The eighth day of her journey greeted the traveler with a sky painted in the soft hues of early morning. A sense of achievement from the previous day's ascent to Sunrise Peak still lingered in her heart, filling her with a quiet confidence. Today, she was to venture into the Grove of Resilience, a place known for its ancient trees that stood as symbols of strength and endurance.

The path to the grove meandered through the forest, its floor dappled with patches of sunlight. With each step, she felt a growing connection to the earth beneath her feet, a reminder of the steady and enduring nature of the natural world. In her pocket, she carried a vial of cedarwood oil, its woodsy aroma deep and grounding. She applied a few drops to her wrists, inhaling the scent that seemed to embody the essence of resilience.

As she entered the grove, she was greeted by a cathedral of towering trees. Their trunks were wide and strong, their branches reaching high into the sky. Each tree stood firm, rooted deeply into the earth, yet swaying gracefully with the wind — a dance of strength and flexibility.

She walked among these giants, feeling humbled by their presence. These trees had weathered countless storms, stood through seasons of change, and yet remained steadfast. They were a testament to the power of resilience, of thriving despite challenges and adversities.

In the heart of the grove, she found a clearing bathed in sunlight. Here, she sat down and leaned against one of the trees, its bark rough against her back. She closed her eyes, allowing the cedarwood oil's scent to fill her senses. In this moment of stillness, she reflected on her own life, on the times she had faced challenges and how she had responded to them.

She thought about her financial struggles, the times when she felt overwhelmed by debt and uncertainty. Like these trees, she had weathered those times, remaining rooted in her determination to overcome them. She envisioned herself as resilient as these trees, standing firm in the face of financial storms, adapting, and growing through them.

Then, she reflected on her relationships. There had been moments of conflict, misunderstanding, and even loss. But like the trees that bend without breaking, she had learned to be flexible, to give and take without losing her core. She saw herself nurturing her relationships with this newfound resilience, building connections that were both strong and adaptable.

Her personal growth, too, had its seasons of change. There were times of rapid growth and times of rest. The trees around her, with their rings marking years of experience, reminded her that growth was a continuous process, with periods of rapid development and times of quiet endurance.

Opening her eyes, she looked up at the canopy above. The leaves whispered softly, a symphony of resilience. Each leaf, each branch, each tree in the grove was a story of survival and strength.

She spent the day in the grove, walking among the trees, touching their bark, listening to their stories. She collected fallen leaves and twigs, symbols of the resilience all around her. The cedarwood oil's fragrance was a constant companion, grounding her thoughts and reinforcing her connection to the enduring strength of nature.

As the sun began to set, casting long shadows across the grove, she knew it was time to leave.

She felt a profound sense of gratitude for the lessons of the day. The Grove of Resilience had shown her the beauty of enduring strength, the importance of staying rooted in one's values while adapting to life's changes.

That night, as she lay in her tent, the scent of cedarwood lingering in the air, she felt a renewed sense of purpose. She had learned from the trees the true meaning of resilience — not just the ability to withstand challenges but to thrive through them.

The journey ahead would undoubtedly present more challenges, but she was ready. Armed with the lessons from the Grove of Resilience and the grounding presence of cedarwood, she was prepared to face life's storms with strength and grace.

Day 9: The Bridge of Forgiveness

Theme: Practicing Forgiveness and Letting Go
Essential Oil: Jasmine – for emotional healing.
Scenario: Crossing a bridge that requires letting go of past hurts and practicing forgiveness.

On the ninth day, as dawn broke with a palette of soft pastels, the traveler embarked on her journey with a heart imbued with the lessons of resilience from the Grove. Today, she was to cross the Bridge of Forgiveness, a symbolic passage known in the enchanted forest for its power to heal and renew. This bridge was not just a physical structure but a metaphor for the journey of reconciliation and letting go of past grievances.

The path to the bridge wove through a part of the forest she hadn't explored before. The air was filled with the subtle sounds of nature, each step forward a reminder of the journey she had undertaken, not just through the forest but within herself. In her pocket, she carried a vial of jasmine oil, its fragrance sweet and soothing, known for its ability to heal emotional wounds and promote forgiveness.

As she approached the bridge, its structure emerged through the mist, an elegant arch spanning a serene river below. The wood was old and worn, yet held a certain grace, as if it had absorbed the stories and pains of those who had walked across it before. She paused at the entrance, applying the jasmine oil to her pulse points, the floral scent enveloping her in a sense of calm and clarity.

Stepping onto the bridge, she felt a wave of emotions wash over her. This was a place where one confronted the hurts of the past, where forgiveness was both sought and given. The river below flowed gently, a symbol of the passage of time and the possibility of renewal.

She thought of the relationships in her life that had been strained or broken. Memories of arguments, misunderstandings, and hurt feelings surfaced. With each step, she allowed herself to feel these emotions fully, the jasmine oil a comforting presence, guiding her through this process of emotional release.

Midway across the bridge, she paused, looking down at the water. She thought of a particular relationship that had caused her much pain — a friendship that had ended in harsh words and unresolved tensions. She realized that holding onto this pain served no purpose but to weigh her down.

Breathing in the scent of jasmine, she mentally extended forgiveness to her friend, letting go of the bitterness and hurt. She also sought forgiveness for her own part in the conflict, acknowledging that healing required forgiving oneself as well.

As she continued her walk, she felt a lightness in her heart, as if an invisible burden had been lifted. The act of forgiving, both others and herself, was liberating. She understood that forgiveness was not about condoning hurtful actions but about freeing oneself from the grip of resentment.

Reaching the other side of the bridge, she took a moment to reflect on her journey across. The bridge had been a passage through her past grievances, a path to emotional freedom. The jasmine oil's soothing fragrance had been her companion, a balm to her emotional wounds.

For the rest of the day, she explored the area around the bridge, the sense of peace and renewal staying with her. She sat by the river, writing in her journal, capturing the insights and emotions of the day. She wrote about the power of forgiveness, how it heals and transforms, and about the strength it takes to let go of the past.

As evening fell, and the sky turned a deep shade of twilight blue, she made her way back to her camp. The scent of jasmine lingered in the air, a reminder of the profound journey she had undertaken on the Bridge of Forgiveness.

That night, as she lay in her tent, she felt a profound sense of wholeness. The journey across the bridge had been challenging, stirring deep emotions, but it had also been a journey of healing. She had crossed not just a physical bridge but had also bridged the gaps in her heart, opening a path to renewed relationships and inner peace.

The traveler fell asleep to the gentle sound of the river, its waters a lullaby of continual flow and transformation. She knew that the journey ahead would bring new challenges, but she was now equipped with the power of forgiveness, ready to face the future with a heart unburdened by the past.

Day 10: The Garden of Gratitude

Theme: Cultivating Gratitude
Essential Oil: Ylang-Ylang – for appreciation and positivity.
Scenario: Tending a garden, where each plant represents an aspect of life to be grateful for.

As the tenth morning dawned with a sky blushing in delicate shades of pink and orange, the traveler awoke with a heart lighter than ever before. The journey across the Bridge of Forgiveness had been a profound experience of healing and letting go. Today, she was to visit the Garden of Gratitude, a mystical place within the enchanted forest known for its serene beauty and the transformative power of thankfulness.

The path to the garden was lined with lush greenery, the air vibrant with the songs of birds and the gentle rustling of leaves. With each step, she felt a growing sense of peace and anticipation. In her hand, she clutched a small bottle of ylang-ylang oil, its fragrance sweet and uplifting, evoking feelings of joy and warmth. She applied a drop to her temples, the floral scent enveloping her in a sense of well-being and contentment.

As she entered the garden, she was greeted by an explosion of colors. Flowers of every hue bloomed in abundance, their petals unfurling towards the sun. The garden was an assortment of life, each plant and flower a testament to the beauty and richness of nature.

In the center of the garden stood a magnificent tree, its branches laden with blossoms. Beneath it was a small pond, its surface a perfect mirror reflecting the sky and the surrounding flora.

Here, in this tranquil oasis, she sat down, taking in the beauty around her, the ylang-ylang oil amplifying her sense of gratitude.

She closed her eyes, taking deep, slow breaths, allowing the essence of the garden and the ylang-ylang to fill her senses. In her mind, she began to recount the blessings in her life, each thought a petal in the garden of her gratitude.

First, she thought of her journey in the enchanted forest. She was grateful for the lessons each day had brought, for the strength she had discovered within herself, and for the transformation she was experiencing. The challenges and the triumphs, the moments of doubt and the bursts of revelation – each was a gift that had contributed to her growth.

Then, she reflected on her relationships. She was thankful for the people in her life, for the love and support they offered. She thought of the friends who had stood by her, the family members who had offered guidance, and even the strangers who had shown kindness along her journey. Each person had touched her life in a meaningful way.

Her thoughts turned to her personal achievements and the progress she had made towards her goals. She was grateful for her resilience in the face of financial struggles, for the courage to mend strained relationships, and for the dedication to her personal growth. Each step forward was a reason to be thankful.

As she opened her eyes, the garden seemed even more vibrant. The colors were richer, the air fresher, and the beauty more pronounced. She realized that gratitude had the power to transform how she viewed the world, turning what was ordinary into something extraordinary.

She spent the day wandering the garden, touching the flowers, and feeling the grass beneath her feet. The ylang-ylang oil's fragrance was a constant reminder of the beauty of life and the abundance of blessings that surrounded her.

In the late afternoon, as the sun began to dip below the horizon, bathing the garden in a warm, golden light, she found a quiet spot by the pond. Here, she took out her journal and began to write, capturing the essence of the day. She wrote about the power of gratitude, how it shifted her perspective, and filled her life with joy and abundance.

That evening, as she lay in her tent, the scent of ylang-ylang lingering in the air, she felt a profound sense of peace and fulfillment. The Garden of Gratitude had opened her eyes to the myriad of blessings in her life, teaching her that gratitude was not just an expression of thanks but a way of living.

She fell asleep to the gentle symphony of the garden, the night air sweet with the fragrance of flowers. She knew that the journey ahead would bring new challenges, but she also knew that with gratitude in her heart, she could face them with positivity and grace.

Day 11: The Orchard of Opportunity

Theme: Recognizing Opportunities
Essential Oil: Grapefruit – for inspiration and spontaneity.
Scenario: Discovering an orchard where each fruit represents a new opportunity, learning to recognize and seize them.

On the eleventh day, as the morning sun cast a gentle golden glow over the forest, the traveler awoke with a heart brimming with gratitude from her time in the Garden. Today's journey would lead her to the Orchard of Opportunity, a place renowned in the enchanted forest for its ability to reveal new paths and possibilities. It was a place where the fruits of opportunity grew in abundance, each ripe with potential and promise.

The path to the orchard meandered through a part of the forest she hadn't explored yet. The air was alive with the anticipation of discovery, each step forward a venture into the unknown. In her hand, she carried a vial of grapefruit oil, its scent bright and energizing. She applied a few drops to her wrists, the citrus aroma invigorating her senses, filling her with a sense of eagerness and readiness to embrace new opportunities.

As she entered the orchard, she was greeted by rows upon rows of trees, each laden with fruits of various hues and sizes. The sight was magnificent, a lush landscape of abundance. The grapefruit oil's scent seemed to amplify the vibrancy of the orchard, each breath a reminder of the endless possibilities that life offered.

She walked among the trees, marveling at the variety of fruits, each representing a different opportunity or path. There were fruits she recognized, symbolizing familiar opportunities related to her current goals and aspirations. But there were also fruits that were strange and unfamiliar, representing paths and possibilities she had never considered.

In the heart of the orchard, she found a serene spot under a large tree with the most unusual fruits. Here, she sat down, the fragrance of grapefruit oil mingling with the sweet aroma of the orchard. She closed her eyes, taking deep breaths, allowing the essence of the orchard to guide her thoughts.

She began to ponder the opportunities in her life. The familiar fruits reminded her of her ongoing goals – her financial stability, nurturing relationships, and personal growth. She felt a renewed commitment to these paths, the lessons from the previous days fueling her determination.

But then, her mind turned to the unfamiliar fruits, the unknown opportunities. She realized that her journey in the enchanted forest was also about exploring new paths, about being open to possibilities she had never considered. Perhaps there were aspects of her life, latent talents, or hidden desires waiting to be discovered and nurtured.

She thought about the potential for new career paths, for learning new skills, or even exploring new hobbies. Each unknown fruit in the orchard was a symbol of these unexplored opportunities. The grapefruit oil's invigorating scent encouraged her to think outside her comfort zone, to be bold and curious.

Opening her eyes, she looked at the orchard with a sense of wonder. She picked a few of the unfamiliar fruits, each a commitment to exploring a new opportunity. She tasted one, its flavor unique and delightful, a metaphor for the joy of discovering new aspects of oneself.

She spent the day in the orchard, exploring, tasting, and sometimes just sitting in contemplation. The orchard was not just a place of abundance but also a space of reflection and exploration. The scent of grapefruit oil was a constant reminder to stay open and receptive to the opportunities that life presented.

As the sun began to set, casting a warm, amber light through the trees, she made her way back to her camp. Her heart was full of excitement for the new paths she had discovered and the possibilities that lay ahead.

That night, as she lay in her tent, the fragrance of grapefruit still lingering in the air, she felt a profound sense of adventure and optimism. The Orchard of Opportunity had opened her eyes to the vast potential within and around her. She had learned that opportunities were not just external prospects but also internal revelations.

She fell asleep with a smile, dreaming of the paths she would explore and the opportunities she would seize. She knew that the journey ahead would be filled with new adventures and discoveries, and she was ready to embrace them all with an open heart and an eager spirit.

Day 12: The Stream of Simplicity

Theme: Finding Joy in Simplicity
Essential Oil: Chamomile – for tranquility and simplicity.
Scenario: A gentle stream teaches the beauty of a simple, uncluttered life, emphasizing the joy in simple pleasures.

On the twelfth morning, as the first rays of sunlight filtered through the trees, casting a soft light on the forest floor, the traveler prepared for the day's journey. Her heart was still buoyant from the discoveries in the Orchard of Opportunity, a place that had opened her eyes to new possibilities. Today, she was to find the Stream of Simplicity, a hidden gem within the enchanted forest known for its clarity and tranquility, a place where one could embrace the joy of a simple, uncluttered life.

The path to the stream was less trodden, winding through dense thickets and overgrown ferns. The air was fresh with the scent of pine and earth, a reminder of the forest's ever-present beauty and mystery. In her hand, she held a vial of chamomile oil, its fragrance gentle and calming. She applied a few drops to her neck, the soothing scent enveloping her in a sense of peace and grounding her in the present moment.

As she journeyed deeper into the forest, the sounds of the world grew faint, replaced by the soft rustling of leaves and the distant sound of flowing water. The simplicity of nature around her was a stark contrast to the complexities of the life she had known outside the forest. Each step on this path was a step towards embracing a simpler, more meaningful existence.

Finally, she reached the Stream of Simplicity. It flowed gently through the forest, its waters clear and pure, reflecting the blue of the sky and the green of the surrounding foliage. The sight of the stream was like a balm to her soul, its simplicity a stark reminder of what truly mattered in life.

She sat by the stream, dipping her feet into the cool water, letting its gentle flow wash over her. The chamomile oil's aroma mingled with the fresh scent of the water, creating an atmosphere of serene simplicity. Here, in this peaceful setting, she began to reflect on her life, on the clutter that filled it — not just physical clutter, but also the clutter of unnecessary worries, commitments, and distractions.

She thought about her financial goals. In her pursuit of stability and security, had she complicated her life with unnecessary desires and material possessions? The stream's clear waters urged her to strip away the superfluous, to focus on what was essential.

Her thoughts turned to her relationships. She realized that the most meaningful connections were often the simplest ones, based on honesty, presence, and love. Like the stream, these relationships didn't need embellishments; they were perfect in their simplicity.

And then, she pondered her personal growth. In her quest for self-improvement, had she lost sight of the joy in simple pleasures? The stream reminded her that sometimes, growth meant slowing down, appreciating the moment, and finding contentment in the little things.

The day passed as she sat by the stream, immersed in thoughts and occasionally writing in her journal. The chamomile oil's calming scent was a constant reminder to embrace simplicity, to let go of the unnecessary, and to focus on the essence of life.

As the sun began to dip below the horizon, casting a golden glow over the stream, she felt a profound sense of clarity and peace. The Stream of Simplicity had taught her that a simple life was not about having less but about being more — more present, more mindful, and more appreciative of the present moment.

That evening, as she lay in her tent, the scent of chamomile lingering in the air, she felt a sense of liberation. She had let go of the complexities that had burdened her and embraced the beauty of simplicity. The stream had shown her a different way of living, one that was richer, deeper, and more fulfilling.

She fell asleep to the gentle sound of the stream, its melody a lullaby of simplicity and peace. She knew that the journey ahead would continue to challenge and transform her, but she was ready. With the lessons of the Stream of Simplicity in her heart, she was prepared to live a life filled with more meaning, more joy, and more gratitude.

Day 13: The Echoing Valley

Theme: Listening to Inner Wisdom
Essential Oil: Sandalwood – for grounding and introspection.
Scenario: In a valley where echoes resonate, learning to listen to one's inner voice and intuition.

As dawn's early light crept over the horizon, painting the sky in soft hues of lavender and gold, the traveler stirred from her slumber. Her soul still resonated with the tranquility from the Stream of Simplicity, carrying with her the lessons of living a life focused on the essential joys. Today's path was leading her to the Echoing Valley, a mystical part of the enchanted forest known for its ability to amplify inner wisdom and voice.

The journey to the valley took her through parts of the forest she hadn't ventured into before. With each step, she felt an increasing sense of introspection, as if the forest itself was guiding her towards deeper self-awareness. In her pocket, she carried a vial of sandalwood oil, its fragrance rich and grounding, known for enhancing mental clarity and introspection. She applied a few drops to her temples, the woody scent centering her thoughts and preparing her for the day's introspective journey.

As she descended into the valley, the air grew cooler, and a profound silence surrounded her, broken only by the occasional bird call or rustle of leaves. The valley was surrounded by high cliffs, their surfaces rugged and ancient. In the heart of the valley, a serene lake lay still, its surface mirroring the surrounding cliffs and sky.

She found a comfortable spot by the lake and sat down, the scent of sandalwood oil filling her senses. Here, in the heart of the Echoing Valley, she closed her eyes and began to focus inward, tuning into her inner voice, often drowned out by the noise of everyday life.

She reflected on her journey thus far, the lessons learned, and the changes she had undergone. The valley, with its echoing cliffs, seemed to magnify her thoughts, allowing her to hear them more clearly. She thought about her aspirations and the doubts that sometimes clouded her judgment. Here, in this space of clarity, she sought to listen to her inner wisdom, the part of her that knew her true potential and path.

The sandalwood oil's scent acted as a conduit, deepening her introspective state. She pondered her financial goals, seeking guidance from within on the best path forward. Her inner voice spoke of patience, perseverance, and the importance of making decisions aligned with her values.

Then, she turned her attention to her relationships. In the silence of the valley, she asked herself what she truly sought from her connections with others. The answers came flowing, echoing around her — authenticity, mutual respect, and unconditional love. The valley was not just echoing her thoughts but was also amplifying her understanding of what truly mattered in her relationships.

Her personal growth, too, was a subject of deep reflection. The valley, with its serene lake and echoing cliffs, encouraged her to listen to her heart's desires. She explored her passions, her fears, and her dreams. The sandalwood oil helped her sift through these reflections, finding the nuggets of truth and wisdom within.

As the day passed, she remained by the lake, sometimes writing in her journal, at other times simply sitting in contemplation. The valley, with its unique ability to echo and clarify thoughts, was a powerful catalyst for self-discovery.

As the sun began to set, casting a warm glow over the valley, she felt a profound sense of enlightenment. The Echoing Valley had served as a mirror, reflecting her deepest thoughts and feelings, allowing her to listen to and understand her inner wisdom.

That evening, as she made her way back to her camp, the fragrance of sandalwood still lingering, she felt a deep connection with herself. She had journeyed into her inner landscape, guided by the echoing whispers of the valley and the grounding presence of sandalwood.

Lying in her tent, under a canopy of stars, she felt a sense of peace and clarity. The journey through the Echoing Valley had been a journey of listening — to her inner voice, her heart, and her soul. She had learned the importance of introspection and self-awareness in navigating the path of life.

She fell asleep to the memories of the day, the echoes of her own wisdom lulling her into dreams. She knew that the journey ahead would continue to challenge her, but she also knew that with the lessons from the Echoing Valley, she was better equipped to listen to her inner guidance and follow the path that resonated with her soul.

Day 14: The Field of Abundance

Theme: Cultivating an Abundance Mindset
Essential Oil: Patchouli – for grounding and prosperity.
Scenario: A lush field demonstrates the richness of an abundance mindset, contrasting scarcity thinking.

On the fourteenth day, as the first light of dawn illuminated the forest with a golden hue, the traveler embarked on her next leg of the journey with a soul enriched by the introspective experiences of the Echoing Valley. Today's path would lead her to the Field of Abundance, a wondrous part of the enchanted forest known for its endless expanse of lush greenery and vibrant life. This field was a symbol of abundance and prosperity, reflecting the unlimited potential and richness of the universe.

The journey to the field was a transition from the dense, introspective atmosphere of the valley to the open, expansive energy of the plains. The air was fresh and invigorating, filled with the promise of new insights and discoveries. In her satchel, she carried a vial of patchouli oil, its deep, earthy aroma a perfect complement to the day's theme of abundance. She anointed her wrists with the oil, its grounding scent setting the tone for a day of exploration into the nature of prosperity.

As she entered the field, she was greeted by a breathtaking sight. The field stretched as far as the eye could see, covered in a myriad of wildflowers, tall grasses, and scattered groves of fruit-bearing trees. The vibrant colors and the sweet fragrance of the flora created an atmosphere of sheer abundance, a stark reminder of nature's generosity and richness.

Walking through the field, the traveler felt a sense of awe and gratitude. The patchouli oil's fragrance seemed to enhance her awareness of the abundance surrounding her. She realized that abundance was not just a physical state but also a mindset, an openness to recognizing and receiving the bounties of life.

She found a spot under a large oak tree, its branches laden with acorns, and sat down to reflect on the concept of abundance in her own life. She pondered her financial goals, now seeing them not just as a pursuit of wealth but as a journey towards creating and acknowledging abundance in all its forms.

Her thoughts turned to her relationships. She realized that abundance in connections meant more than just the number of friends or the frequency of interactions. It was about the depth of connections, the richness of experiences shared, and the mutual support and love that flourished.

Then, she contemplated her personal growth. The field, with its endless expanse and diversity, symbolized the limitless possibilities for learning, exploration, and self-expression. She recognized that her growth was not limited by external circumstances but was boundless, fueled by her curiosity and passion.

As the day unfolded, she wandered through the field, taking in its beauty and diversity. She picked wildflowers, each a symbol of a different aspect of abundance in her life. The patchouli oil's grounding scent was a constant reminder to stay connected to the earth and to appreciate the abundance that sprang from it.

In the late afternoon, as she sat by a small stream that meandered through the field, she took out her journal. Inspired by the surroundings, she wrote about the lessons of abundance. She wrote about shifting her focus from scarcity to abundance, from what was lacking to what was overflowing in her life.

As the sun began to set, casting a warm, golden light over the field, she felt a profound sense of fulfillment and peace. The Field of Abundance had opened her eyes to the endless possibilities and richness of life. She had learned that abundance was not just about material wealth but was also about richness in experiences, relationships, and self-discovery.

That evening, as she lay in her tent, the scent of patchouli lingering in the air, she felt overwhelmed with a sense of prosperity and gratitude. The journey through the Field of Abundance had been a journey of recognizing and embracing the unlimited potential that life offered.

She fell asleep with a heart full of thankfulness, dreaming of the abundant life that awaited her. She knew that the journey ahead would bring new challenges and opportunities, but she also knew that with the lessons of abundance, she was equipped to embrace them with an open heart and a spirit of gratitude.

Day 15: The Path of Empathy

Theme: Developing Empathy and Compassion
Essential Oil: Geranium – for emotional balance and empathy.
Scenario: A path where each step allows feeling and understanding others' emotions, fostering empathy.

The fifteenth day of the traveler's journey in the enchanted forest broke with a sky streaked in pastel colors, heralding another day of profound exploration and growth. After her enlightening experience in the Field of Abundance, she felt a deeper connection to the world around her and a heightened sense of awareness. Today, she was to walk the Path of Empathy, a trail known for its mystical ability to deepen understanding and compassion towards others.

The path to this unique part of the forest took her through a landscape that gradually became more lush and vibrant. The air around her was filled with the gentle sounds of nature, a harmonious symphony that seemed to attune her more closely to the feelings and energies around her. In her pocket, she carried a vial of geranium oil, its floral and sweet aroma known for fostering emotional balance and empathy. She applied the oil to her pulse points, its scent enveloping her in a feeling of warmth and sensitivity towards the feelings of others.

As she ventured deeper, the path brought her to a grove where the trees seemed to whisper secrets of ancient wisdom. The leaves rustled in the wind, each whispering a story of joy, sorrow, love, and loss. Here in the Path of Empathy, the traveler felt as if she could hear the silent stories of the forest, each plant and creature sharing their experiences with her.

She found a serene spot by a babbling brook and sat down, the fragrance of the geranium oil mingling with the fresh, earthy scent of the forest. Closing her eyes, she allowed herself to open up to the emotions and stories around her. She could sense the joy of the birds singing in the trees, the quiet strength of the towering oaks, and the playful curiosity of the small creatures scurrying in the underbrush.

The Path of Empathy was not just a physical trail but a journey into the hearts and experiences of others. The traveler began to reflect on her relationships, seeing them now through a lens of deeper empathy and understanding. She thought of her family and friends, each with their own struggles and triumphs. The geranium oil's soothing presence helped her to feel more deeply connected to their emotions, understanding their perspectives and experiences.

Her thoughts then turned to the people she had met during her journey in the forest. She remembered their faces, their words, and the emotions they had shared. With each memory, she felt a growing sense of empathy, a deeper connection to the shared human experience.

As she sat by the brook, she also pondered her own emotions and how they connected her to others. She realized that empathy was not just about understanding others but also about recognizing the common feelings and experiences that bind us all. The geranium oil seemed to enhance this realization, its fragrance a reminder of the interconnectedness of all life.

Throughout the day, she walked the path, sometimes sitting in quiet contemplation, other times reaching out to touch the bark of a tree or the petals of a flower, each touch a gesture of understanding and connection. The path was teaching her that empathy was an active practice, a conscious choice to connect with others and share in their emotional journey.

As the sun began to set, casting a soft golden light through the trees, she felt a profound sense of gratitude for the day's journey. The Path of Empathy had opened her heart to the beauty of shared emotions and the power of understanding and compassion.

That evening, as she lay in her tent, the scent of geranium still lingering in the air, she felt a deep sense of peace and connection. The journey through the Path of Empathy had been a journey of the heart, teaching her the importance of empathy in building meaningful relationships and a compassionate life.

She fell asleep with a heart full of empathy and love, dreaming of the connections she would continue to make and nurture. She knew that the journey ahead would continue to challenge her, but she also knew that with the lessons of empathy, she was better equipped to understand and connect with the world around her.

Day 16: The Hill of Positive Aspirations

Theme: Positive Thinking and Affirmations
Essential Oil: Bergamot – for upliftment and positivity.
Scenario: Climbing a hill where positive affirmations grow like wildflowers, learning the power of positive thinking.

On the sixteenth day, as the dawn unfurled a beam of light over the enchanted forest, the traveler arose, her spirit enriched by the profound lessons of empathy from the day before. Today, she was to ascend the Hill of Positive Aspirations, a place revered for its ability to inspire and uplift those who journeyed to its summit. It was a place where the power of positive thinking and affirmations was magnified, turning hopes and dreams into tangible visions.

The path to the hill was a gradual ascent, winding through a landscape that shimmered with the morning dew. The air was crisp, filled with an energy that seemed to pulse with potential and possibility. In her satchel, she carried a vial of bergamot oil, its fragrance bright and uplifting, known for its ability to enhance mood and promote positivity. She applied the oil behind her ears, its citrus aroma invigorating her senses and setting the tone for a day of positive thinking and aspirations.

As she began her climb, the hill revealed its unique beauty. Wildflowers of various hues peppered the green expanse, and the sound of birds singing in harmony filled the air. The beauty of the hill was a physical manifestation of the positive energy that it harbored, a reminder of the beauty that positive thoughts and aspirations could bring into life.

Reaching a plateau, she paused to take in the view. The forest stretched out below her, a vast and verdant expanse that spoke of life's endless possibilities. The scent of bergamot oil mingled with the fresh air, reinforcing her sense of optimism and hope.

Here, she sat down, drawing her journal from her satchel. Inspired by the surroundings, she began to write down her aspirations, infusing each goal with positivity and belief. She wrote about her financial ambitions, not just as mere goals but as manifestations of her capability and hard work. She framed each aspiration in positive language, seeing her financial stability as a reality waiting to happen.

Her thoughts then turned to her relationships. On the Hill of Positive Aspirations, each relationship was a source of joy and growth. She envisioned her connections with family and friends deepening, filled with mutual understanding, support, and love. The bergamot oil's uplifting scent encouraged her to envision her relationships in their best light, thriving and enriching her life.

She also reflected on her personal growth. With the expansive view before her, she saw her journey of self-improvement as a path filled with discovery, joy, and fulfillment. She wrote down her aspirations to learn, create, and explore; each goal imbued with a sense of excitement and positive anticipation.

As the day progressed, she continued her climb to the summit of the hill. With each step, her spirits lifted, buoyed by the bergamot oil's bright fragrance and the natural beauty surrounding her. The hill seemed to echo her positive thoughts, amplifying them, making them feel more real and attainable.

Reaching the summit, she was greeted by a breathtaking view. The horizon stretched far and wide, a symbol of the limitless potential of her aspirations. Here, she took a moment to meditate, focusing on her goals and the positive energy she wished to attract.

Surrounded by the beauty of the hill and the energizing scent of bergamot, she felt as if her aspirations were already in the process of coming true. The power of positive thinking was palpable here, turning her hopes and dreams into something she could almost touch and feel.

As the sun began to descend, painting the sky in hues of orange and purple, she made her way back down the hill, her heart light and her mind filled with positive thoughts. The journey up the Hill of Positive Aspirations had been a journey of hope and optimism, a testament to the power of a positive mindset.

That evening, as she lay in her tent, the aroma of bergamot still lingering in the air, she felt a profound sense of joy and anticipation. The Hill of Positive Aspirations had shown her that her thoughts had the power to shape her reality, that positivity was a force that could bring her dreams to life.

She fell asleep with a smile, dreaming of the bright future that awaited her. She knew that the journey ahead would be filled with challenges, but she also knew that with her positive aspirations and the lessons from the hill, she was equipped to face them with optimism and determination.

Day 17: The Misty Lagoon of Trust

Theme: Learning to Trust the Journey
Essential Oil: Myrrh – for trust and transformation.
Scenario: Navigating a misty lagoon, learning to trust the journey even when the destination isn't clear.

As the dawn of the seventeenth day painted the sky in a kaleidoscope of colors, the traveler awakened with a heart full of the positive aspirations she had nurtured on the Hill. Today, she was to venture into the Misty Lagoon of Trust, a mystical and secluded part of the enchanted forest known for its serene waters and the profound sense of trust and surrender it instilled in those who visited.

The path to the lagoon was veiled in a gentle mist, creating an ethereal atmosphere that seemed to transport her to another world. The air was cool and moist, carrying with it the scent of wet earth and green leaves. In her hand, she held a vial of myrrh oil, its aroma deep and resinous, known for its properties of grounding and promoting spiritual trust. She anointed her forehead with the oil, its scent instilling in her a sense of calm and a readiness to embrace the lessons of trust that the day would bring.

As she walked deeper into the mist, the forest around her took on a surreal quality. The trees and plants appeared as silhouettes; their outlines softened by the enveloping fog. The path became less defined, and she realized that to reach the lagoon, she would need to rely on her intuition and inner guidance rather than her sight.

The journey was a metaphor for the moments in life when the way forward was unclear, and the only option was to trust in oneself and the journey. The myrrh oil's grounding fragrance was a constant reminder of her inner strength and the trust she had in herself and the path she had chosen.

Eventually, the forest opened up to reveal the Misty Lagoon. It was a breathtaking sight – a vast expanse of still water, its surface a perfect mirror reflecting the mist and the sky above. The lagoon was surrounded by tall reeds and flowering plants, adding to the sense of isolation and tranquility.

She found a spot by the water's edge and sat down, letting the peacefulness of the lagoon wash over her. Here, in this secluded haven, she began to reflect on the role of trust in her life. She thought about the times she had faced uncertainty and how trust had been her anchor, guiding her through the unknown.

She pondered her financial journey, realizing that trust in her abilities and decisions was crucial to achieving her goals. The lagoon, with its calm and steady presence, was a reminder that trusting the flow of life could bring a sense of peace and assurance, even in the face of financial challenges.

Her thoughts then turned to her relationships. Trust was the foundation of every meaningful connection, the invisible bond that held them together. She thought about the importance of trusting others but also the necessity of being trustworthy herself. The myrrh oil's presence reinforced this realization, its fragrance a symbol of the deep and sacred bond of trust.

She also contemplated the trust she placed in her personal growth journey. Like navigating through the mist to reach the lagoon, her path of self-improvement was often shrouded in uncertainty. But she had learned to trust the process, to believe in her ability to grow and evolve, even when the end result was not immediately visible.

As she sat by the lagoon, lost in thought, the mist began to lift slowly, revealing the lush beauty of the surroundings. It was as if the lagoon was unveiling itself to her, a reward for her trust in the journey to get here.

The rest of the day was spent in quiet contemplation by the water. The lagoon was a teacher in its own right, its stillness a lesson in trust and surrender. The myrrh oil was her companion throughout, its grounding aroma a constant reminder of the stability and peace that trust in oneself and the journey could bring.

As evening approached, and she made her way back through the now clearing mist, she felt a profound sense of gratitude and peace. The journey to the Misty Lagoon of Trust had been a journey into the heart of trust itself, teaching her the importance of believing in the unseen and the power of surrendering to the flow of life.

That night, as she lay in her tent, the scent of myrrh still lingering in the air, she felt a sense of deep trust and contentment. She had learned that trust was not just a feeling but a choice, a decision to believe in oneself, in others, and in the journey of life, even when the path was not clear.

She fell asleep with a heart full of trust, dreaming of the paths she would walk and the waters she would cross. She knew that the journey ahead would be filled with unknowns, but she also knew that with trust as her guide, she was ready to face whatever lay ahead.

Day 18: The Circle of Community

Theme: Embracing Community and Support
Essential Oil: Clary Sage – for clarity and communal harmony.
Scenario: Finding a circle of trees symbolizing community, understanding the strength in seeking and offering support.

As the eighteenth day dawned, casting a soft, warm light through the trees of the enchanted forest, the traveler stirred from her restful slumber, filled with a sense of trust and peace from her experience at the Misty Lagoon. Today, she was to explore the Circle of Community, a sacred place within the forest known for its emphasis on the importance of connection, support, and unity.

The path to the Circle of Community took her through a dense part of the forest, where the trees grew close together, their branches intertwined, creating a natural archway that seemed to welcome her into a space of togetherness and belonging. In her satchel, she carried a vial of clary sage oil, its herbaceous and slightly floral aroma known for enhancing clarity and communal harmony. She applied the oil to her wrists, its scent instilling in her a sense of openness and readiness to connect with the essence of community.

As she ventured deeper, the forest opened up to reveal a clearing where a circle of stones lay. Each stone was different – some large, some small, all shapes and sizes – yet they were arranged in perfect harmony, creating a circle that spoke of unity and balance. The clearing was alive with the energy of togetherness, the trees around standing like silent sentinels, guarding this sacred space.

Sitting on one of the stones, the traveler took a moment to absorb the atmosphere. The clary sage oil's fragrance heightened her sense of connection to the world around her. She reflected on the various communities she had been a part of – her family, friends, and even the fleeting connections she had made during her journey in the forest. Each community, she realized, had played a crucial role in her life, offering support, love, and a sense of belonging.

The Circle of Community was not just a physical space but a symbol of the interconnectedness of all beings. She thought about how each individual in a community was like a stone in the circle – unique and different, yet essential to the completeness and balance of the whole. The clary sage oil seemed to echo this sentiment, its harmonizing properties a reminder of the beauty of diverse elements coming together in unity.

She contemplated her role in her communities. How had she contributed? How had she supported others? In what ways had she allowed herself to be supported? The Circle of Community encouraged her to not only reflect on these questions but also to recognize the importance of giving and receiving support.

As the day progressed, she remained in the clearing, sometimes walking around the circle of stones, touching each one, acknowledging the significance of each member in a community. The clary sage oil was a constant companion, its scent a reminder to maintain clarity in her intentions and interactions within her communities.

The sun began its descent, casting long shadows across the clearing. The day in the Circle of Community had been a profound experience, teaching her the value of connection, the strength of support, and the beauty of unity in diversity.

As she made her way back to her camp, the fragrance of clary sage accompanying her, she felt a deep sense of gratitude for the communities in her life. She realized that no one is an island, that each person is part of a larger web of relationships and connections.

That evening, as she lay in her tent, the scent of clary sage still lingering, she felt a renewed commitment to nurture her relationships and to actively contribute to her communities. The Circle of Community had shown her that every individual has the power to impact and strengthen the collective, and that together, a community can face any challenge and achieve any goal.

She fell asleep with a heart full of appreciation for the circles of community she was a part of, dreaming of the ways she could continue to connect, support, and grow with them. She knew that the journey ahead would bring new opportunities to forge connections and build communities, and she was ready to embrace them with an open heart and a spirit of collaboration.

Day 19: The Mountain of Victory

Theme: Celebrating Small Victories
Essential Oil: Cypress – for momentum and transition.
Scenario: Climbing a mountain, marking and celebrating each small victory along the ascent.

On the nineteenth day, as the early morning sun bathed the forest in a golden light, the traveler set out with a sense of connection and purpose, her spirit enriched by the experiences at the Circle of Community. Today, she would ascend the Mountain of Victory, a majestic peak in the heart of the enchanted forest known for its symbolism of achievement and the celebration of life's milestones.

The path to the mountain was steep and rugged, weaving through dense foliage and over rocky terrain. The air grew crisp and cool as she climbed higher, each step a testament to her determination and strength. In her satchel, she carried a vial of cypress oil, its fresh and invigorating aroma known for encouraging momentum and transition. She applied the oil to her neck and wrists, its scent instilling in her a sense of resolve and a readiness to embrace the challenges of the climb.

As she ascended, the traveler reflected on her journey so far. Each day in the enchanted forest had been a step towards self-discovery, a victory in its own right. The path to the summit of the Mountain of Victory was not just a physical challenge but a metaphor for her personal journey, a climb towards her goals and aspirations.

The cypress oil's energizing fragrance seemed to propel her forward, each breath a reminder of her progress and the victories she had already achieved. She thought about her financial goals, the steps she had taken to achieve stability and security. She realized that each wise decision, each act of saving and budgeting, was a victory on her financial journey.

Her thoughts then turned to her relationships. She had mended bridges, nurtured connections, and opened her heart to new friendships. Each of these was a victory in the realm of relationships, a testament to her capacity for love, understanding, and empathy.

She also considered her personal growth. The journey in the forest had been one of profound self-improvement, with each day bringing new lessons and insights. She had faced her fears, embraced change, and pursued her passions. Every step of growth was a victory, a celebration of her evolving self.

The climb became more challenging as she neared the summit, but she pressed on, driven by the cypress oil's uplifting scent and the symbolic importance of reaching the peak. The mountain, with its daunting presence, was a reminder that victories often required perseverance and resilience.

Finally, after hours of climbing, she reached the summit. The view from the top was breathtaking – a panoramic vista of the entire enchanted forest, stretching out in all its splendor. Standing there, on the Mountain of Victory, she felt a rush of accomplishment and pride.

She took a moment to celebrate her victories, both big and small. She thought about the obstacles she had overcome, the goals she had achieved, and the personal growth she had experienced. The cypress oil's scent empowered her, reinforcing the feeling of triumph and the importance of acknowledging and celebrating one's achievements.

As the sun traveled across the sky, she explored the summit, taking in the beauty and serenity of the view. She found a quiet spot and took out her journal, writing down her thoughts and reflections. She wrote about the victories she had celebrated, the lessons learned, and the sense of accomplishment she felt.

As evening approached and the sun began to set, casting a warm, orange glow over the mountain, she prepared for her descent. The journey down the mountain was a time for reflection, a chance to internalize the lessons of the day.

That night, as she lay in her tent, the scent of cypress still lingering, she felt a deep sense of gratitude and fulfillment. The Mountain of Victory had been a journey of celebration, a recognition of her achievements and the journey she had undertaken.

She fell asleep with a heart full of joy, dreaming of the mountains she would climb in the future. She knew that the journey ahead would bring new challenges, but she also knew that with each step, she was achieving victories, both big and small, on her journey through life.

Day 20: The Garden of Self-Care

Theme: Importance of Self-Care and Self-Love
Essential Oil: Rose – for love and compassion.
Scenario: Tending a garden of self-care, nurturing the soul with acts of self-love and care.

As the dawn of the twentieth day broke, casting a soft, serene light over the enchanted forest, the traveler awoke with a heart still resonating with the triumphs celebrated atop the Mountain of Victory. Today, she was set to embark on a journey to the Garden of Self-Care, a sacred place within the forest known for its healing energies and nurturing environment, a haven for self-reflection, restoration, and rejuvenation.

The path to the garden was a gentle walk through a part of the forest she had not yet explored. With each step, she felt a growing sense of tranquility and peace, as if the very air around her was preparing her for the nurturing experience of the garden. In her satchel, she carried a vial of rose oil, its fragrance rich and soothing, known for its properties of love, compassion, and emotional healing. She anointed her heart and wrists with the oil, its floral aroma enveloping her in a blanket of care and warmth.

As she entered the garden, she was greeted by a sight of breathtaking beauty. The garden was a lush blanket of vibrant colors and fragrances, with flowers in full bloom, lush greenery, and a symphony of bird songs and gentle breezes. The garden was a living embodiment of care and nurturing, each plant and flower a reminder of the importance of nurturing oneself.

Walking through the garden, the traveler felt a deep connection with the surrounding nature.

The rose oil's fragrance heightened her sense of self-awareness and compassion. She realized that self-care was not a luxury but a necessity, an essential part of her journey towards self-discovery and growth.

She found a quiet spot by a bubbling brook and sat down, letting the peacefulness of the garden wash over her. Here, in this serene oasis, she began to reflect on her journey so far. She thought about the challenges she had faced, the victories she had celebrated, and the lessons she had learned. The garden, with its nurturing presence, encouraged her to take a moment to care for herself, to acknowledge her needs and tend to them with kindness and compassion.

The rose oil's scent inspired her to think about her physical well-being. She acknowledged the importance of taking care of her body, the vessel that carried her through this journey of life. She made a mental note to nourish her body with healthy food, restful sleep, and physical activity, to keep it strong and resilient.

Her thoughts then turned to her emotional health. The garden, with its tranquil ambiance, was a reminder of the importance of tending to her emotional garden. She realized the need to give herself space to feel and express her emotions, to practice self-compassion, and to seek support when needed. The rose oil's soothing presence was a balm to her soul, encouraging her to embrace her emotions with understanding and love.

She also contemplated her mental well-being. The journey in the forest had been mentally stimulating and at times challenging. She recognized the importance of giving her mind time to rest and rejuvenate, to engage in activities that brought her joy and relaxation. The garden, with its peaceful environment, was a perfect place to unwind and clear her mind.

As the day unfolded, she wandered through the garden, sometimes sitting in quiet contemplation, other times engaging in gentle activities that nurtured her body, mind, and soul. She practiced yoga on a grassy knoll, meditated by the brook, and journaled under the shade of a large oak tree. The rose oil's fragrance was a constant companion, its essence a reminder to practice self-love and care.

In the late afternoon, as she lay on a bed of soft grass, looking up at the sky through the canopy of leaves, she felt a profound sense of well-being and contentment. The Garden of Self-Care had been a sanctuary, a place to reconnect with herself and nurture all aspects of her being.

As evening approached, and she made her way back to her camp, the fragrance of rose still lingering on her skin, she felt a deep sense of gratitude for the day's experiences. The garden had taught her the importance of self-care, of taking the time to nurture and care for herself, just as she would for a cherished garden.

That night, as she lay in her tent, held in the comforting scent of rose, she felt a renewed sense of vitality and peace. The journey through the Garden of Self-Care had been a journey of love – love for herself, for her journey, and for the life she was creating.

She fell asleep with a smile, dreaming of the beautiful garden and the lessons it had imparted. She knew that the journey ahead would be filled with new adventures and challenges, but she also knew that with the practice of self-care, she was well-equipped to face them with strength, resilience, and grace.

Day 21: The Starlit Clearing of Dreams

Theme: Realizing Dreams and Aspirations
Essential Oil: Neroli – for ambition and purpose.
Scenario: A starlit clearing where dreams manifest, learning to turn aspirations into reality.

As the twenty-first day dawned in the enchanted forest, the traveler awoke in her tent, still feeling the comforting fragrance of rose from her rejuvenating experience in the Garden of Self-

Care. Today, she was to journey to the Starlit Clearing of Dreams, a mystical and secluded area known for its night-time beauty and for inspiring dreamers to pursue their deepest aspirations.

The path to the clearing was a meandering trail through dense parts of the forest, leading her away from the familiar into uncharted territories. The air was crisp, filled with a sense of mystery and anticipation. In her satchel, she carried a vial of neroli oil, its sweet, citrusy aroma known for its ability to stimulate the mind and encourage ambition and purpose. She applied the oil to her temples, its fragrance uplifting her spirit and preparing her for a day of exploration into the world of dreams and aspirations.

As the day progressed and she walked deeper into the forest, the sky above began to transform into a canvas of twilight, adorned with the first twinkling stars. The deeper she ventured, the more the forest seemed to awaken with nocturnal life, the sounds of night creatures and the rustling of leaves under the moonlight creating a symphony of the night.

Eventually, she reached the Starlit Clearing of Dreams. It was a breathtaking sight – an open space in the forest canopy allowed a clear view of the night sky, the stars shining brightly above, their light reflecting in a small, serene pond at the center of the clearing. The clearing was a place of peace and wonder, a perfect backdrop for contemplating dreams and the future.

Sitting by the pond, the traveler gazed up at the stars, the neroli oil's fragrance enhancing her sense of clarity and vision. Here, in this magical setting, she began to reflect on her dreams, the aspirations that she had carried in her heart, some of them long buried under the responsibilities and routines of life.

The Starlit Clearing was not just a physical space but a gateway to the realm of possibilities. She thought about her career aspirations, envisioning a path that aligned with her passions and strengths. The stars above seemed to encourage her to dream big, to reach for what truly fulfilled her.

Her thoughts then turned to personal dreams, those aspirations that transcended career and finances. She dreamed of travel, of experiencing different cultures and landscapes. She envisioned herself pursuing hobbies that brought her joy, learning new skills, and embracing new experiences. The neroli oil's inspiring scent seemed to whisper to her that no dream was too big or too small.

She also pondered her dreams for her relationships. She envisioned deep and meaningful connections, a life shared with loved ones filled with laughter, support, and shared adventures. The starlit sky above was a reminder that, like the stars, each relationship had its unique glow, contributing to the beauty of her life.

As the night deepened, she lay back on the grass, the entire clearing and sky above her becoming an immersive experience. The stars seemed to dance, each one a symbol of a dream or aspiration. The neroli oil's aroma assured her, each breath a reminder of her potential and the limitless possibilities that life offered.

She spent the entire night in the clearing, sometimes in quiet contemplation, other times writing in her journal by the soft glow of the moon. She wrote about her dreams, detailing them with as much clarity as the stars above her. She wrote about the steps she could take to make these dreams a reality, the neroli oil fueling her ambition and creativity.

As dawn approached, painting the sky in hues of pink and blue, she felt a profound sense of purpose and direction. The Starlit Clearing of Dreams had been a sanctuary for her aspirations, a place where she could connect with her deepest desires and the universe's boundless potential.

That morning, as she made her way back to her camp, the fragrance of neroli lingering on her skin, she felt a renewed sense of optimism and determination. The journey through the Starlit Clearing had been a journey of dreaming and envisioning a future filled with fulfillment and joy.

She fell asleep just as the first light of dawn kissed the forest, her heart full of dreams and her mind alive with possibilities. She knew that the journey ahead would bring new challenges, but she also knew that with the clarity and inspiration from the clearing, she was ready to pursue her dreams with courage and conviction.

Day 22: The Winds of Change

Theme: Adapting to Change Gracefully
Essential Oil: Juniper Berry – for adaptability and protection.
Scenario: Winds that change the landscape, teaching adaptability and the grace to embrace change.

As the twenty-second day dawned in the enchanted forest, the traveler awoke from her dream-filled slumber, her mind still echoing with the visions of the Starlit Clearing. Today, she was to journey through the Winds of Change, a unique area of the forest known for its shifting breezes and the ability to inspire adaptability and embrace transformation.

The path to this region of the forest meandered through changing landscapes, from dense wooded areas to open meadows. The air around her seemed to be in constant motion, gentle gusts of wind bringing with them the scents of various flora. In her satchel, she carried a vial of juniper berry oil, its crisp, clean aroma known for its properties of protection and adaptability. She applied the oil to her temples and wrists, its invigorating scent sharpening her senses and preparing her for the day's lessons.

As she ventured deeper into the Winds of Change, she noticed the trees and plants around her swaying rhythmically with the wind. It was as if the forest itself was teaching her the art of bending and swaying with change, rather than resisting it. The juniper berry oil's fragrance seemed to reinforce this lesson, reminding her of the strength in flexibility and the grace in adaptation.

The wind grew stronger as she progressed, its howls and whispers telling tales of transformation and renewal. She saw leaves being carried away by the wind, a symbol of letting go of the old to make way for the new. The traveler realized that change was an inevitable and natural part of life, a force that could bring about growth and new beginnings if embraced.

She found a spot in a clearing where the wind danced around her, lifting her hair and caressing her face. Here, she closed her eyes and allowed herself to be swept by the winds of change, contemplating the areas of her life where change was occurring or needed.

She thought about her financial goals and how adapting to new strategies and ideas could lead to greater stability and prosperity. The wind seemed to whisper encouragement, urging her to be open to new methods of managing her finances, to learn from the past but not be bound by it.

Her thoughts then turned to her relationships. Change was a constant in human interactions, sometimes challenging but always an opportunity for deeper understanding and connection. She contemplated how being adaptable in her relationships, being open to new perspectives and experiences, could strengthen her bonds with others.

She also reflected on her personal growth. The journey in the enchanted forest had been one of continuous change and transformation. She realized that her growth was about embracing change, about being open to new experiences and lessons that shaped her into a more rounded and evolved individual. The juniper berry oil's aroma was a reminder that change was not something to fear but to welcome as a catalyst for growth.

As she sat in the clearing, the wind bringing with it scents from different parts of the forest, she felt a profound connection with the nature of change. She understood that like the wind, change was constant and could be harnessed for positive transformation.

The day passed with her exploring different parts of the Winds of Change, each area offering new insights and perspectives. She wrote in her journal, capturing the lessons and reflections of the day, the scent of juniper berry accompanying her thoughts.

As evening approached and the wind settled into a gentle breeze, she felt a sense of peace and readiness. The journey through the Winds of Change had taught her the importance of being adaptable, of flowing with the winds of life rather than standing rigid against them.

That night, as she lay in her tent, the fragrance of juniper berry still lingering, she felt a renewed sense of resilience and flexibility. She had learned that in the dance with change, there was beauty and strength, and that by embracing change, she opened herself to a world of possibilities and growth.

She fell asleep with a heart open to the winds of change, dreaming of the paths she would explore and the transformations she would embrace. She knew that the journey ahead would bring new changes, but she also knew that with the lessons of the Winds of Change, she was ready to meet them with grace and adaptability.

Day 23: The Sunlit Path of Joy

Theme: Finding Everyday Joy
Essential Oil: Mandarin – for cheerfulness and joy.
Scenario: A path bathed in sunlight, discovering the joy in everyday moments and the beauty of the present.

On the twenty-third day, as the morning sun cast a warm, embracing light through the foliage of the enchanted forest, the traveler set forth with a newfound appreciation for adaptability and resilience, her spirit buoyed by the lessons from the Winds of Change. Today, she was to tread the Sunlit Path of Joy, a radiant and warm part of the forest known for its ability to awaken the simplest and most profound form of happiness.

The path to this special area of the forest took her through a mosaic of light and shadow, where beams of sunlight pierced through the canopy, creating patterns of gold and green on the forest floor. The air was filled with the sweet songs of birds, and the vibrant colors of nature seemed to be in a state of celebration. In her pocket, she carried a vial of mandarin oil, its fragrance sweet and cheerful, known for its uplifting and joyous properties. She applied the oil to her pulse points, the citrus aroma infusing her with a sense of light-heartedness and anticipation for the day's joys.

As she walked, the forest gradually opened up to a wide, sun-drenched path. The sunlight bathed everything in a golden hue, the flowers and leaves shimmering as if in delight. The Sunlit Path of Joy was not just a place but a state of being, a reminder that joy often lay in the simplest of things.

Embraced by the warmth of the sun and the sweet scent of mandarin, the traveler felt a surge of simple, unadulterated joy. She realized that happiness was not always about grand achievements or significant events; it was also about appreciating the beauty of the present moment, the beauty of nature, and the small pleasures of life.

Walking along the path, she began to reflect on the sources of joy in her life. She thought about the moments that brought her happiness, the activities that made her heart sing, and the people who brought smiles to her face. The Sunlit Path of Joy encouraged her to acknowledge and cherish these sources of happiness, to make space for them in her everyday life.

She pondered her financial journey, realizing that while stability and security were important, true joy often came from experiences rather than material possessions. The sunlight seemed to agree, its golden beams a reminder of the richness of life beyond the material.

Her thoughts then turned to her relationships. She understood that joy in relationships came from sharing, caring, and simply being together. The laughter, the conversations, and even the shared silences were sources of immense happiness. The mandarin oil's cheerful scent reminded her to nurture these joyful interactions, to create and cherish happy memories with loved ones.

She also contemplated the joy in her personal growth. Each step of her journey in the forest had brought its own form of happiness – the thrill of discovery, the peace of self-acceptance, and the satisfaction of overcoming challenges. The path, bathed in sunlight, was a metaphor for her journey, illuminating the joy in growth and learning.

Throughout the day, she engaged in activities that brought her joy. She danced in the sunlight, laughed with the birds, and lay in the grass, looking up at the sky, letting the simple act of being in nature fill her with happiness. The mandarin oil's uplifting fragrance was a constant companion, enhancing each joyful moment.

As the sun began to dip below the horizon, bathing the path in a soft, warm glow, she felt a profound sense of gratitude and happiness. The Sunlit Path of Joy had taught her the importance of recognizing and embracing the joy in everyday life, of finding happiness in the simple and the ordinary.

That evening, as she settled into her camp, the scent of mandarin still lingering, she felt a deep sense of contentment and peace. The journey through the Sunlit Path of Joy had been a celebration of life's simplest pleasures, a reminder that joy was always around her, waiting to be acknowledged and experienced.

She fell asleep with a smile, her dreams filled with the golden light of the path and the simple joys of life. She knew that the journey ahead would bring its share of challenges, but she also knew that with the lessons from the Sunlit Path of Joy, she could always find happiness along the way.

Day 24: The Moonlit Glade of Reflection

Theme: Reflecting on Growth and Progress
Essential Oil: Lavender – for calm reflection.
Scenario: A tranquil glade under moonlight, reflecting on personal growth and the journey thus far.

As dusk fell upon the enchanted forest on the twenty-fourth day, the traveler prepared for a night-time journey, a departure from her usual morning excursions. Tonight, she was to visit the Moonlit Glade of Reflection, a mystical and serene part of the forest illuminated by the soft glow of the moon, known for its power to evoke deep introspection and contemplation.

The path to the glade was a tranquil walk under the starry sky, the forest around her bathed in the ethereal light of the moon. The air was cool and clear, carrying with it the promise of introspective revelations. In her satchel, she carried a vial of lavender oil, its fragrance calm and soothing, known for its ability to promote reflection and inner peace. She applied the oil to her temples, its aroma enveloping her in a sense of tranquility and preparing her for the reflective journey ahead.

As she entered the Moonlit Glade, she found herself in an open space surrounded by ancient trees, their leaves whispering secrets in the gentle night breeze. The moon hung low in the sky, casting a silver light over the glade, creating a landscape that seemed otherworldly. The glade was a haven for self-exploration, a place where one could delve into the depths of their soul under the watchful eye of the moon.

Sitting on a fallen log, the traveler gazed up at the moon, the lavender oil's fragrance heightening her sense of introspection. Here, in the stillness of the night, she began to reflect on her journey so far. The Moonlit Glade was not just a physical location but a symbol of the reflective journey within, a journey into the heart of her experiences, emotions, and thoughts.

She contemplated the changes she had undergone since entering the enchanted forest. The journey had been transformative, each day presenting new challenges and learnings. The moonlit setting encouraged her to look deeper, to acknowledge the growth and the shifts in her perspective. The lavender oil's soothing presence was a balm to her introspective journey, offering a sense of calm as she explored the depths of her inner self.

Her thoughts turned to her aspirations and the dreams she had envisioned on the Starlit Clearing. The moon's soft light seemed to encourage her to revisit these dreams, to reflect on their meaning and the steps she needed to take to realize them. The glade, with its serene ambiance, was a perfect backdrop for planning and envisioning the future.

She also reflected on her relationships, considering the connections she had strengthened and the new bonds she had formed. The quiet of the glade allowed her to think about the qualities she valued in her relationships, the lessons she had learned from others, and the kind of friend, family member, and companion she aspired to be. The lavender oil's calming scent reminded her to approach her relationships with gentleness and understanding.

As the night deepened, she walked around the glade, sometimes sitting in quiet contemplation, other times lying on her back, looking up at the stars. The Moonlit Glade of Reflection was a sanctuary for her thoughts, a place where she could be alone with her reflections, yet feel a profound connection with the universe.

The moon traversed the sky, casting shifting shadows and light across the glade. The traveler wrote in her journal by the moonlight, capturing the insights and revelations of the night. She wrote about her inner discoveries, the emotions she had explored, and the clarity she had gained.

As dawn approached, painting the sky in hues of pink and blue, she felt a sense of fulfillment and peace. The journey through the Moonlit Glade of Reflection had been a journey of introspection, a night spent in communion with her deepest self.

That morning, as she made her way back to her camp, the fragrance of lavender still clinging to her, she felt a renewed sense of understanding and purpose. The journey through the glade had taught her the importance of taking time for reflection, of looking inward to gain insight and direction.

She fell asleep just as the first light of dawn kissed the forest, her heart full of the reflections of the night and her mind clear with the insights gained. She knew that the journey ahead would bring new experiences and challenges, but she also knew that with the lessons of the Moonlit Glade, she was equipped to face them with a deeper understanding of herself and her path.

Day 25: The Fountain of Forgiveness

Theme: Deepening the Practice of Forgiveness
Essential Oil: Pine – for renewal and forgiveness.
Scenario: A fountain where the waters heal old wounds, deepening the understanding and practice of forgiveness.

On the twenty-fifth day, as the early light filtered through the trees of the enchanted forest, the traveler stirred from her rest, her mind still echoing with the introspections from the Moonlit Glade. Today, she was to visit the Fountain of Forgiveness, a sacred and healing site deep within the forest, known for its ability to facilitate deep emotional healing and the letting go of past hurts.

The path to the fountain was a labyrinthine trail through lush undergrowth and ancient trees, each step taking her further into the heart of the forest. The air was heavy with the scent of moss and earth, a reminder of the forest's timeless wisdom and healing powers. In her satchel, she carried a vial of pine oil, its fresh, clean aroma known for its properties of renewal and emotional release. She anointed her heart and temples with the oil, its scent grounding her and preparing her heart for the process of forgiveness.

As she neared the Fountain of Forgiveness, she could hear the sound of water gently cascading, a soothing symphony that seemed to wash over her soul even before she laid eyes on it. The fountain itself was a marvel – a natural spring that flowed into a basin surrounded by a variety of flowering plants, each bloom a testament to the rejuvenating power of forgiveness.

Sitting by the fountain, the traveler gazed into the clear water, the pine oil's fragrance enhancing her sense of clarity and purpose. Here, in the presence of the healing waters, she began to reflect on the concept of forgiveness, both forgiving others and seeking forgiveness for herself.

The journey through the enchanted forest had brought many memories to the surface – some filled with joy and love, others tinged with regret and sorrow. The Fountain of Forgiveness was a place to confront these emotions, to acknowledge the hurts and to release them into the healing waters.

She thought about relationships where misunderstandings and mistakes had created distance and pain. The sound of the flowing water encouraged her to let go of the resentment and anger, to understand the perspectives of others, and to offer forgiveness, not as an act of condonation but as a step towards healing.

She also contemplated moments where she had erred, where her actions or words had caused pain to others. The pine oil's scent reminded her of the importance of seeking forgiveness, of owning up to her mistakes and making amends. The act of seeking forgiveness was an act of courage and honesty, a step towards reconciliation and inner peace.

As the day unfolded, she spent time meditating by the fountain, sometimes writing in her journal, other times simply watching the water flow, each droplet a symbol of release and renewal. The Fountain of Forgiveness was not just a physical space but a journey into the depths of her heart, a place to heal and to be reborn from the waters of compassion and understanding.

The experience at the fountain was transformative. With each moment spent in reflection, she felt the weight of past hurts and grievances lifting from her shoulders. The pine oil's aroma was a constant reminder of the freshness and clarity that forgiveness brought.

As evening approached, and the light turned golden, filtering through the trees and reflecting in the fountain's waters, she felt a profound sense of liberation and peace. The journey to the Fountain of Forgiveness had been a journey of emotional cleansing, a process of letting go of the past and embracing the present with an open and healed heart.

That night, as she lay in her tent, the scent of pine still lingering, she felt a deep sense of gratitude for the experiences of the day. The journey through the Fountain of Forgiveness had taught her the power of forgiveness in healing and transforming lives, her own and those of others.

She fell asleep with a heart lighter than it had been in years, her dreams serene and soothing. She knew that the journey ahead would bring new challenges and experiences, but she also knew that with the lessons of forgiveness, she was equipped to face them with a heart free from the burdens of the past.

Day 26: The Meadow of Mindfulness

Theme: Overcoming Fear and Embracing Courage
Essential Oil: Ginger – for courage and presence.
Scenario: A forest where shadows represent fears, learning to face and overcome them with courage.

On the twenty-sixth day, as the first light of dawn gently awakened the enchanted forest, the traveler rose, her spirit still imbued with the profound sense of peace from the Fountain of Forgiveness. Today, she was destined for the Meadow of Mindfulness, a sacred expanse within the forest that whispered of tranquility and the art of presence. This meadow, known for its lush greenery and vibrant life, served as a sanctuary for those seeking to deepen their connection with the present moment and embrace the fullness of life.

The journey to the meadow was a gradual unfolding of beauty and serenity, with the path winding through areas where the morning mist clung to the leaves and the light played hide and seek with the shadows. The air was a blend of fresh, earthy scents and the subtle fragrance of wildflowers, creating an atmosphere of calm and clarity. In her satchel, she carried a vial of vetiver oil, its rich, grounding aroma perfect for enhancing mindfulness and introspection. She applied the oil to her pulse points, its scent enveloping her in a sense of balance and grounding, preparing her mind and soul for the day's exploration.

As she entered the Meadow of Mindfulness, she was greeted by an expanse of lush grasses dotted with wildflowers, a jumble of color and life under the soft morning sun. A gentle breeze stirred the air, carrying with it the songs of birds and the rustling of leaves, a natural symphony that invited her to pause and listen, to truly be present.

Sitting by the edge of a tranquil stream that meandered through the meadow, the traveler closed her eyes, drawing in deep breaths filled with the vetiver oil's aroma. In this moment of stillness, she became acutely aware of the life teeming around her – the gentle hum of insects, the whisper of the grass, the rhythmic flow of the stream. Each sound, each sensation, was a reminder of the beauty of the present moment, a call to embrace the here and now with openness and awareness.

The Meadow of Mindfulness was more than a physical location; it was a manifestation of the state of being fully engaged in the present. She reflected on how often her thoughts wandered to the past or drifted towards the future, missing the richness and depth of the current moment. The meadow, with its serene and vibrant energy, taught her the value of mindfulness – the practice of being fully immersed in the experience of now, of savoring each sensation and cherishing each moment.

She wandered through the meadow, her senses heightened by the grounding presence of the vetiver oil. She touched the flowers, feeling the texture of their petals; she observed the insects as they moved with purpose; she listened to the melody of the stream, each note a reminder of life's constant flow and the beauty of embracing its rhythm.

Her journey through the enchanted forest had been a practice in mindfulness, each day a lesson in being present and engaged with her experiences and emotions. She realized that mindfulness was not merely a technique but a way of living, a path to experiencing life in its fullest, richest form.

As the sun climbed higher, casting a warm glow over the meadow, she found a shaded spot under a grand oak tree. Here, she engaged in mindful practices – meditation, deep breathing, and gentle yoga movements. Each practice was enhanced by the vetiver oil's scent, anchoring her in the present and deepening her connection to her inner self.

In the quiet of the afternoon, she sat journaling by the stream, capturing her thoughts and reflections. She wrote about the insights gained in the meadow, about the peace that comes from living mindfully, and about her intentions to carry this mindfulness into every aspect of her life.

The day in the Meadow of Mindfulness came to a close with a deep sense of fulfillment and serenity. As she made her way back to her camp, the earthy fragrance of vetiver accompanying her, she felt a profound connection to the present moment, to the forest, and to her own journey.

That night, as she lay in her tent, immersed in the tranquil scent of vetiver, she felt a deep sense of gratitude for the day's experiences. The Meadow of Mindfulness had been a sanctuary of presence, teaching her the transformative power of fully engaging with the here and now.

She drifted into sleep with a peaceful heart, her dreams a continuation of the day's serenity. She knew that the journey ahead would offer new experiences and challenges, but with the practice of mindfulness, she was prepared to meet them with a calm, centered spirit.

Day 27: The Valley of Visions

Theme: Practicing Mindfulness and Presence
Essential Oil: Basil – for mental clarity and awareness.
Scenario: A meadow that heightens the senses, teaching the art of mindfulness and living in the moment.

As the twenty-seventh day dawned with a palette of soft morning hues painting the sky, the traveler awoke with a sense of calm and presence instilled by her experiences in the

Meadow of Mindfulness. Today, she was to venture into the Valley of Visions, a mystical part of the forest revered for its power to evoke clarity of thought and inspire visionary thinking.

The journey to the valley was a descent through rolling hills and dense thickets, each step taking her deeper into a world of introspection and contemplation. The forest here was ancient, its trees towering and majestic, creating a canopy that filtered the sunlight into a mosaic of light and shadow. In her satchel, she carried a vial of frankincense oil, its rich, woody aroma known for enhancing spiritual connection and insight. She anointed her forehead and wrists with the oil, its scent grounding her in a state of readiness to explore the depths of her visions and aspirations.

As she entered the Valley of Visions, she was greeted by a landscape that seemed to stretch beyond the physical realm. The valley was enveloped in a gentle mist that softened the edges of the world, creating an atmosphere that was ethereal and otherworldly. The air was charged with an energy of potential and possibility, the essence of the valley inviting her to delve into the realm of her deepest dreams and visions.

Finding a secluded spot by a serene pond at the heart of the valley, the traveler sat down, the fragrance of frankincense enveloping her in an aura of introspection. The still waters of the pond served as a mirror, reflecting not just the physical surroundings but also offering a glimpse into the depths of her soul.

Here, in the tranquility of the valley, she began to explore her visions for the future. The frankincense oil's aroma heightened her sense of connection to her inner wisdom, guiding her thoughts towards clarity and purpose. She pondered her life's path, considering the direction she wished to take, both personally and professionally. The valley, with its mystical energy, encouraged her to think beyond the confines of the ordinary, to envision a life that was fulfilling and aligned with her deepest values.

She contemplated the impact she wished to have on the world, her aspirations to contribute and make a difference. The Valley of Visions was a place where such dreams took on a vivid and tangible form, where the barriers between imagination and reality seemed to blur.

Her thoughts then turned to her personal growth and development. She envisioned herself continuing on a path of self-discovery, embracing new experiences, and learning from each twist and turn of her journey. The frankincense oil's grounding presence reminded her that every vision for the future was rooted in the growth and learning of the present.

As the day unfolded, she walked along the paths of the valley, each step a meditation on her aspirations and dreams. She engaged in moments of quiet reflection by the pond, sometimes writing in her journal, at other times simply gazing into the waters, lost in her thoughts.

The valley, with its misty ambiance and serene beauty, was a crucible for her visions. Here, she felt free to dream without limits, to explore possibilities that lay beyond the horizon of her current reality. The scent of frankincense was a constant companion, its aroma a bridge between the tangible world and the realm of dreams and visions.

As evening approached, and the valley was bathed in the soft glow of the setting sun, she felt a profound sense of clarity and direction. The journey through the Valley of Visions had been a journey into the future, a glimpse into the potential of her life's path.

That night, as she lay in her tent, the fragrance of frankincense hanging in the air, she felt a deep sense of connection with her dreams and a renewed sense of purpose. The valley had shown her that her visions were more than mere fantasies; they were signposts guiding her toward her true path.

She fell asleep with a heart full of hope and eyes full of stars, her dreams a continuation of the visions she had explored in the valley. She knew that the journey ahead would bring challenges and uncertainties, but she also knew that with the clarity and insight gained from the Valley of Visions, she was equipped to navigate her path with confidence and conviction.

Day 28: The Canopy of Courage

Theme: Aligning with Core Values
Essential Oil: Thyme – for releasing and aligning with values.
Scenario: A valley where each path represents a core value, aligning actions with true values.

As the morning sun cast a golden glow over the enchanted forest on the twenty-eighth day, the traveler embarked on her journey with a heart full of the visions and insights gleaned from the Valley of Visions. Today, she was to traverse the

Canopy of Courage, a towering forest within the enchanted woods known for its ability to imbue travelers with bravery and resolve.

The path to the canopy was a gradual ascent, leading her through a dense underbrush into a realm where the trees reached towards the heavens, their branches interlocking to form a magnificent canopy above. The air here was fresh and invigorating, filled with the songs of birds and the rustling of leaves. In her satchel, she carried a vial of cedarwood oil, its aroma woody and reassuring, known for its properties of instilling strength and courage. She applied the oil to her pulse points, its scent bolstering her spirit and preparing her for the challenges of the day.

As she ventured deeper into the Canopy of Courage, she was struck by the majesty and grandeur of the trees. They stood as ancient guardians, their trunks wide and strong, their leaves whispering secrets of endurance and resilience. The canopy above filtered the sunlight into a kaleidoscope of light and shadow, creating an ambiance that was both awe-inspiring and humbling.

Sitting at the base of one of the great trees, the traveler felt a deep connection to the strength and stability it represented. The cedarwood oil's grounding fragrance enhanced this connection, reminding her that true courage was rooted in inner strength and conviction.

Here, in the embrace of the Canopy of Courage, she began to reflect on the moments in her journey when she had faced fear and uncertainty. The canopy, with its protective and empowering presence, encouraged her to confront those fears, to acknowledge them, and to find the courage within herself to overcome them.

She pondered the fears that had held her back – fear of failure, fear of the unknown, and even fear of her own potential. The Canopy of Courage was a testament to the power of facing one's fears, of standing tall and steadfast in the face of adversity. The cedarwood oil's scent was a reminder that courage was not the absence of fear but the decision to act in spite of it.

Her thoughts then turned to her aspirations and the challenges that lay ahead in achieving them.

She realized that to follow her dreams, she would need to harness the courage to take risks, to step out of her comfort zone, and to embrace the journey with all its uncertainties. The canopy, with its resilient and enduring trees, stood as a symbol of the bravery required to pursue one's dreams.

As she walked through the Canopy of Courage, touching the bark of the trees and looking up at the interlacing branches, she felt her resolve strengthening. Each step was a reinforcement of her courage, a commitment to move forward despite the fears and doubts that might arise.

The day passed with her exploring the canopy, engaging in moments of contemplation and writing in her journal. She wrote about her fears and how she planned to face them, about the courage she had found in the forest, and about her determination to pursue her dreams with bravery and resolve.

As evening approached, and the canopy was bathed in the soft light of the setting sun, she felt a profound sense of empowerment and readiness. The journey through the Canopy of

Courage had been a journey of inner fortification, a process of awakening the bravery that resided within her.

That night, as she lay in her tent, the scent of cedarwood still lingering, she felt a deep sense of confidence and strength. The canopy had taught her the importance of courage in the face of life's challenges, of standing tall and unyielding like the ancient trees.

She fell asleep with a heart full of determination, her dreams a reflection of the courage she had embraced. She knew that the journey ahead would test her resolve, but she also knew that with the lessons of the Canopy of Courage, she was equipped to face them with bravery and steadfastness.

Day 29: The Labyrinth of Legacy

Theme: Embracing Renewal and New Beginnings
Essential Oil: Lemon Grass – for cleansing and renewal.
Scenario: A river that cleanses old patterns, embracing renewal and the excitement of new beginnings.

On the twenty-ninth day, as the first rays of dawn cast a golden hue over the enchanted forest, the traveler embarked on a journey to the

Labyrinth of Legacy, a profound and introspective part of the woods. Known for its intricate pathways and reflective ambiance, the labyrinth was a place to contemplate one's legacy and the impact of one's life journey.

The path to the labyrinth wound through the forest, leading her deeper into a realm of introspection and contemplation. The air was rich with the scent of ancient earth and old growth, a reminder of the timeless nature of legacy. In her satchel, she carried a vial of myrrh oil, its aroma deep and introspective, known for its connection to wisdom and the weaving of one's life story. She applied the oil to her heart and temples, its fragrance grounding her in the gravity of the day's journey.

As she entered the Labyrinth of Legacy, she found herself surrounded by towering walls of verdant foliage, the paths before her weaving in and out of sight. The labyrinth was a metaphor for the journey of life – full of twists and turns, moments of clarity followed by bouts of uncertainty. The myrrh oil's aroma was a constant reminder of the depth and significance of each choice and step in the weaving of her life's story.

Walking through the labyrinth, the traveler reflected on the concept of legacy – what she would leave behind and how she would be remembered. The quiet rustling of leaves and the soft crunch of the earth beneath her feet provided a rhythmic backdrop to her thoughts. She pondered her actions, her contributions to the world, and the ripples they created in the lives of others.

The labyrinth prompted her to think about the impact of her financial decisions – not just on her life but on the world around her. She contemplated the ways in which her economic choices reflected her values and the legacy she wished to build. The myrrh oil's scent encouraged a deeper understanding of how her financial stewardship could leave a lasting impression.

Her thoughts then turned to her relationships. She considered how her interactions, her love, her compassion, and even her conflicts had shaped her life and the lives of those around her.

The labyrinth, with its complex pathways, mirrored the complexities of human relationships – each turn and twist a different chapter in her relational legacy.

She also reflected on her personal growth and the legacy of her inner journey. Each step in the labyrinth was a step in her own journey of self-discovery, of overcoming challenges, of growing and evolving. The myrrh oil's grounding presence reminded her that her personal legacy was not just about achievements and accolades but also about the person she was becoming, the values she embodied, and the wisdom she shared.

As she navigated the labyrinth, she found moments of clarity where paths intersected, offering brief moments to pause and look back on the journey so far. These moments were opportunities to see the bigger picture, to understand how each piece of her journey contributed to the whole.

Throughout the day, she journaled at various points in the labyrinth, capturing her reflections on legacy, on the mark she wished to leave on the world, and on the stories she wanted to be told. The act of writing in the heart of the labyrinth was a way to crystallize her thoughts, to make tangible the intangible aspects of her legacy.

As the sun began to set, casting long shadows through the labyrinth, she found her way to its center – a clearing with a solitary ancient tree, its branches stretching towards the sky. Here, in the heart of the labyrinth, she felt a profound connection to the past, present, and future – a nexus of time where her legacy felt both rooted in history and stretching into the future.

That evening, as she made her way back to her camp, the scent of myrrh lingering in the air, she felt a deep sense of purpose and intentionality. The journey through the Labyrinth of Legacy had been a journey of understanding the impact of her life, of recognizing the power of her actions, and of envisioning the legacy she wished to create.

She fell asleep with a heart full of aspirations, her dreams a continuation of the day's reflections. She knew that the final day of her journey in the enchanted forest was approaching, but she also knew that with the insights from the Labyrinth of Legacy, she was ready to weave a legacy that reflected her deepest values and aspirations.

Day 30: The Summit of Synthesis

Theme: Living in Prosperity and Gratitude
Essential Oil: Cinnamon – for abundance and gratitude.
Scenario: Reaching the summit, looking back on the journey with gratitude, embracing a life of prosperity and fulfillment.

On the thirtieth and final day of her journey in the enchanted forest, the traveler awoke to a sunrise that painted the sky in brilliant hues of orange and pink. Today, she was to ascend to the

Summit of Synthesis, the highest point in the forest, known as a place of culmination and reflection, where one could integrate the myriad lessons and experiences of their journey.

The path to the summit was a steep and winding ascent, cutting through dense woodland before opening up to rocky outcrops and sparse vegetation. The air grew cooler and sharper as she climbed, a physical reminder of the elevation she was gaining and the culmination of her journey. In her satchel, she carried a vial of rosemary oil, its clear and invigorating aroma known for enhancing memory and mental clarity. She applied the oil to her temples, its scent sharpening her focus and preparing her mind for the day's reflection and synthesis.

As she ascended, the traveler reflected on the journey that had brought her here. Each step upwards was a metaphor for the path she had traversed in the enchanted forest – a journey filled with challenges, learnings, and growth. The rosemary oil's fragrance seemed to unlock the doors to her memories, allowing her to vividly recall the lessons from each day.

She remembered the tranquility of the Whispering Trees, where she learned the power of introspection and the importance of listening to the wisdom within. She recalled the courage she found in the Canopy of Courage, the joy in the Sunlit Path of Joy, and the profound sense of peace in the Meadow of Mindfulness.

The Summit of Synthesis represented the integration of all these experiences, a place where she could weave together the fabric of her journey. It was not just about remembering each lesson but about understanding how they were interconnected, how each experience was a thread that contributed to the fabric of her growth.

The higher she climbed, the more expansive the view became. The forest stretched out below her, a vast and verdant landscape that spoke of her journey's breadth and depth. The rosemary oil's crisp scent kept her mind alert and focused, aiding her in the process of synthesis and integration.

Reaching the summit, she found herself on a plateau that offered a panoramic view of the entire forest. The sight was awe-inspiring, a physical manifestation of the journey she had undertaken. She sat there, on the highest point in the forest, surrounded by the beauty of the world below and the endless sky above.

Here, at the summit, she took time to meditate to allow the synthesis of her experiences to unfold within her. She contemplated the changes she had undergone, the strengths she had discovered, and the wisdom she had gained. The rosemary oil's aroma assured her each breath a reminder of her journey's richness and the interconnectedness of her experiences.

As the day unfolded, she journaled, capturing the essence of her synthesis. She wrote about how each lesson had shaped her and how the experiences in the forest had woven together to form a clearer picture of her path and purpose. The act of writing was a way to solidify her understanding, to make tangible the intangible revelations of her journey.

The summit, with its breathtaking view and serene atmosphere, was a place of profound reflection and understanding. Here, she felt a deep connection with herself and the journey she had embarked upon. The lessons of the forest, now synthesized and integrated, formed a roadmap for her future, guiding her towards a life of purpose, growth, and fulfillment.

As the sun began to set, casting a golden glow over the summit, she felt a sense of completion and wholeness. The journey to the Summit of Synthesis had been a journey of integration, a process of bringing together the many facets of her experiences into a cohesive whole.

That evening, as she descended from the summit, the scent of rosemary accompanying her, she felt a profound sense of gratitude for the journey she had undertaken. The enchanted forest had been a teacher, a guide, and a companion, leading her through a transformative process that had touched every aspect of her being.

She fell asleep under the stars, her heart full of the memories and lessons of the past thirty days. She knew that while her journey in the enchanted forest had come to an end, the journey of her life was continuing, enriched and guided by the experiences and wisdom she had gained.

Conclusion: The Journey Forward

As the traveler stood at the edge of the enchanted forest, where the dense canopy gave way to the open skies of the world beyond, she paused to take a deep, reflective breath. The early morning sun cast a warm, inviting glow over the path ahead, a path that led back to her everyday life, a life she was now prepared to face with a newfound sense of happiness, prosperity, and confidence.

The journey through the forest had been transformative. Each day, each experience had woven into her being a medley of strength, wisdom, and resilience. She felt a surge of gratitude for the lessons learned – for the courage she had discovered within herself in the Canopy of Courage, for the joy she had embraced in the Sunlit Path of Joy, for the peace she had found in the Meadow of Mindfulness, and for the clarity of purpose she had achieved at the Summit of Synthesis.

With the scent of rosemary oil still lingering faintly on her skin, a reminder of her last day in the forest and the synthesis of her experiences, she stepped forward, crossing the threshold from the mystical realm back into the reality of her life. The challenges and stresses of everyday existence awaited her, but she approached them with a new perspective.

Her first steps were deliberate and confident. She had a plan, a vision forged in the Valley of Visions, tempered in the Labyrinth of Legacy, and solidified on the Summit of Synthesis. She knew her path wasn't just about achieving personal goals but also about creating a positive impact on the world around her.

As she made her way through the familiar streets of her city, the hustle and bustle of daily life surrounded her. The noise, the pace, the demands – all were the same, but she was different. She carried within her an oasis of tranquility, a reservoir of strength to draw upon.

Her first actions were grounded in the lessons of the forest. She approached her financial goals with a sense of purpose and clarity, remembering the insights from the Whispering Trees about listening to her inner wisdom. She tackled challenges with the courage she had honed in the Canopy of Courage, no longer deterred by fear or uncertainty.

In her relationships, she brought the empathy and understanding cultivated in the Circle of Community and the Fountain of Forgiveness. She nurtured her connections with love and presence, valuing each moment spent with family, friends, and colleagues.

Her personal growth continued to be a journey of discovery and fulfillment. She pursued her passions with the joy she had embraced in the Sunlit Path of Joy and the mindfulness she had practiced in the Meadow of Mindfulness. She set aside time for self-care, remembering the rejuvenating power of the Garden of Self-Care.

The traveler approached her career and future aspirations with a vision that was clear and focused, guided by the legacy she wished to create and the dreams she had nurtured in the Valley of Visions and the Starlit Clearing. She was no longer daunted by the prospect of change, drawing upon the adaptability she had learned in the Winds of Change.

As days turned into weeks and weeks into months, the traveler found that the happiness, prosperity, and confidence she had cultivated in the enchanted forest were not fleeting but a permanent part of her being. She faced life's challenges with grace and resilience, her heart full of the wisdom and insights from her journey.

The enchanted forest was no longer a physical place she visited, but a part of her, a sanctuary in her heart that she could return to whenever she needed guidance, strength, or peace. Her journey through the forest had ended, but her journey through life – enriched and empowered by her experiences – was just beginning.

She moved forward with a smile, a beacon of positivity and strength, her life a living testament to the transformative power of her journey. In her heart, she carried the forest with her, a reminder that no matter what life brought her way, she was prepared to face it and emerge victorious.

Appendix A

Theme

1. Understanding and Acknowledging Current State
2. Setting Clear, Achievable Goals
3. Understanding the Law of Correspondence
4. Establishing Small, Consistent Habits
5. Visualizing Success and Prosperity
6. Overcoming Limiting Beliefs
7. Embracing a New Perspective
8. Building Resilience and Strength
9. Practicing Forgiveness and Letting Go
10. Cultivating Gratitude
11. Recognizing Opportunities
12. Finding Joy in Simplicity
13. Listening to Inner Wisdom
14. Cultivating an Abundance Mindset
15. Developing Empathy and Compassion
16. Positive Thinking and Affirmations
17. Learning to Trust the Journey
18. Embracing Community and Support
19. Celebrating Small Victories
20. Importance of Self-Care and Self-Love
21. Realizing Dreams and Aspirations
22. Adapting to Change Gracefully
23. Finding Everyday Joy
24. Reflecting on Growth and Progress
25. Deepening the Practice of Forgiveness

26. Overcoming Fear and Embracing Courage
27. Practicing Mindfulness and Presence
28. Aligning with Core Values
29. Embracing Renewal and New Beginnings
30. Living in Prosperity and Gratitude

Appendix B

Thirty Days of Essential Oils

1. Peppermint
2. Lavender
3. Eucalyptus
4. Lemon
5. Rosemary
6. Frankincense
7. Orange
8. Cedarwood
9. Jasmine
10. Ylang-Ylang
11. Grapefruit
12. Chamomile
13. Sandalwood
14. Patchouli
15. Geranium
16. Bergamot
17. Myrrh
18. Clary Sage
19. Cypress
20. Rose
21. Neroli
22. Juniper Berry
23. Mandarin
24. Lavender
25. Pine

26. Ginger
27. Basil
28. Thyme
29. Lemongrass
30. Cinnamon

About the Author

Sydney Brown has spent over thirty-five years in the business world and later in the corporate world. She has learned what works and what doesn't when the goal is to get out of the stale, vanilla world of the generations before us.

She believes that each person has at least one successful business, one book, and one grand adventure in them, but most people don't know how to figure out their best fit, so they stay where they are.

She is a best-selling author, speaker, and coach, helping people reach out of their current situation and reinvent themselves so they can do more than exist and survive while in this great space.

Personally, she's a mom of two adulting children and proudly owns the title of "Crazy Cat Lady" among her friends. After too many years of avoiding living life, she is on a mission to help others identify and begin their own "Great Ascension."

Let's Connect

If you've enjoyed this book, you'll love what else is ahead!

Start out at https://beyourownsolution.com/ and see what you can look forward to.

We have courses, certifications, and life and business focused free groups!

Free Groups:
https://www.facebook.com/groups/fundsfriendsfutures
https://www.facebook.com/groups/shifttimes

Also From TLM Publishing House

FICTION –
Sydney Brown Presents Series
https://www.amazon.com/dp/B0BSBT36HN
The Mall Cadet Series
https://www.amazon.com/gp/product/B0B66MDK3T
All In or Nothing Series
https://www.amazon.com/dp/B0B7FW9W8M
The 7 Wishes Series
https://www.amazon.com/dp/B0B62XJY59
The Deception Series
https://www.amazon.com/dp/B0B5RNQMF1
The Forbidden Love Series (18+)
https://www.amazon.com/dp/B0B5SX24SX
The Essential Witch Chronicles
https://www.amazon.com/dp/B0CKSHS1H1

NONFICTION –
How to Start It Series
https://www.amazon.com/dp/B09Y2QHDPM
Aromatherapy Alchemy
https://www.amazon.com/dp/B0CJ5DD5C1
Foundational Knowledge of All Things Wellness and Success
https://www.amazon.com/dp/B0CL8ZF9K7

www.ingramcontent.com/pod-product-compliance
Lightning Source LLC
LaVergne TN
LVHW020928090426
835512LV00020B/3260